An Introduction To
Australian Wine

AN INTRODUCTION TO
AUSTRALIAN WINE

JAMES HALLIDAY

HarperCollins*Publishers*

This book could not have been written without the friendship and co-operation of countless wine professionals — makers, judges, retailers and connoisseurs — unstintingly extended to me over the past thirty years. If the book helps you understand the magic spell which wine has woven around us all, I shall have repaid that help in some small way.

AN ANGUS & ROBERTSON BOOK
An imprint of HarperCollinsPublishers

First published in Australia in 1992 by
CollinsAngus&Robertson Publishers Pty Limited (ACN 009 913 517)
A division of HarperCollinsPublishers (Australia) Pty Limited
25-31 Ryde Road, Pymble NSW 2073, Australia
HarperCollinsPublishers (New Zealand) Limited
31 View Road, Glenfield, Auckland 10, New Zealand
HarperCollinsPublishers Limited
77-85 Fulham Palace Road, London W6 8JB, United Kingdom
Distributed in the United States of America by
HarperCollins Publishers
10 East 53rd Street, New York NY 10022, USA

National Library of Australia
Cataloguing-in-Publication data:
Halliday, James, 1938-
  An introduction to Australian wine.
  Includes index.
  ISBN 0 207 17437 7.
  1. Wine and wine making – Australia. I. Title.
641.220994.

Cover photograph of James Halliday by Oliver Strewe
Printed in Hong Kong
5 4 3 2 1
96 95 94 93 92

CONTENTS

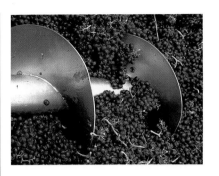

1 INTRODUCTION

'Let us have wine and women, mirth and laughter,
sermons and soda water the day after.' BYRON

If you are to ever really enjoy wine, and through that enjoyment progressively master its many mysteries, you must not allow yourself to be intimidated by it or by experts (real or imagined) who seek to tell you what you should like or dislike.

Wine is fun. Accept it for what it is. Trust what your palate tells you, and wine itself will be the best teacher you can find. It is not necessary that you become an instant expert, capable of bandying the arcane terminology of the wine writer with your friends and guests. Nor is it necessary that you rush out and spend lots of money on expensive bottles before you have become thoroughly comfortable with ordinary wine — the wine you buy in casks or low-priced bottles.

Many regular wine drinkers will happily remain cask drinkers for their entire lives, neither knowing nor caring what grapes were used, where they were grown or how the wine was made. They may find that one brand of cask usually suits their taste better than another, but some will make their choice on the basis of price alone. In many ways, these are the luckiest consumers: wine makes no demands on them, simply representing one of the basic pleasures of a civilised existence.

But for some wine will come to mean much more. Since 1950 there has been a transformation in Australian attitudes to wine and food, partly deriving from factors peculiar to Australia and partly reflecting worldwide changes. The Australian factors were the influx of migrants from Europe, the experiences of servicemen and women during the Second World War, and — progressively through the 1960s and thereafter — the increasing ease and cheapness of overseas travel for teenagers and young adults. All of these factors have led to the Europeanisation of our attitudes to wine and food. The worldwide changes flow from the impact of satellite-relayed television, the continuous growth in world trade of every type of commodity, and the increasing leisure and affluence of the average citizen of the developed nations.

The chart (page 8) showing the increase in table wine consumption (and the decrease in fortified wine consumption) tells part of the tale, but only part. As a teenager in the 1950s I was fortunate to be exposed to fine wine through my parents, and my luck continued during my six years' residency at St Paul's College, Sydney University while I obtained my arts and law degrees: the college had a wine cellar, and we were permitted to have wine twice a week.

But for most other teenagers of the time, wine was a rarity at best. Beer was the commonly consumed alcohol, with spirits and mixed drinks the only alternative at mixed gatherings. What is more, in 1960 there were no regular wine columns in the newspapers, no tastings at

OPPOSITE: The four storey bluestone winery of Craiglee in Victoria was built by James S. Johnston in the 1870s.

7

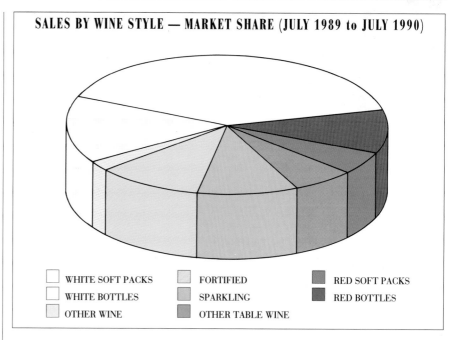

SALES BY WINE STYLE — MARKET SHARE (JULY 1989 to JULY 1990)

WHITE SOFT PACKS   FORTIFIED   RED SOFT PACKS

WHITE BOTTLES   SPARKLING   RED BOTTLES

OTHER WINE   OTHER TABLE WINE

wine shops, no wine lectures and almost no books on wine for the general reader. Walter James, whose books include *Barrell and Book* (1949) and *Wine in Australia* (1955) was a graceful but singular exception, although his writings were in the tradition of the English essayists: gentle, philosophical reflections rather than hard, factual information or precisely articulated opinion.

How different it is today: at the age of twenty I was grappling with the revelation that Shiraz and Hermitage were grape names, yet (confusingly) denoted the same grape. I knew of the Hunter Valley — and had indeed visited it several times — but was only vaguely aware of the existence of other regions apart from the Barossa Valley. Yet I was 'into wine', as the saying goes. The twenty-year-old of today who is 'into wine' will not only not need this book, but could write much of it.

Hopefully, this guide will take you some way down the path I have followed since those early days. How far and how fast is up to you. Do not feel pressured by your peers: be aware that the wine siren has her own magic call, and that she will catch you when you least expect it.

2 WINE: A BRIEF PERSPECTIVE

'Wine brings to light the hidden secrets of the soul.'
HORACE

Wine is one of the most natural of all of the long-life foodstuffs, and has been part of civilisation since 5000 BC. Since that time the basic process of winemaking has remained unchanged: yeasts convert the sugar present in the grapes into alcohol. All that is necessary is to remove the grape skins at the end of fermentation and to give the wine time to naturally clarify itself before it is drawn off for consumption or bottling.

Nothing has to be added to achieve this result: no special equipment is essential, though it is certainly desirable; and if the wine is kept reasonably protected from air (or to be precise oxygen) and is consumed within a few months of being made, no preservatives or other additives are necessary. In other words, made and consumed this way, it is an entirely natural product, and it was this which our ancestors enjoyed 7500 years ago.

Recent archaeological research has provided evidence of winemaking in the Zagros Mountains of western Iran, not far from Iraq, 500 years earlier than previously believed. From here, and from nearby Georgia, winemaking moved west, reaching Egypt and Phoenicia by 3000 BC, thence to Greece by 2000 BC, and on to Italy and North Africa by 1000 BC.

Contrary to common belief, it was the Greeks who first brought vines to France, establishing vineyards near Marseilles around 600 BC and in the Languedoc-Rousillion region around 200 BC. The Romans were the most important influence in the longer term, establishing vines in Bordeaux and the Rhône Valley around 50 AD, and at roughly 100-year intervals thereafter successively in Burgundy, the Loire Valley and Champagne.

The vine has since spread around the world, with major production areas in Western Europe, North and South America, South Africa and Australasia. In terms of production, Australia is not a major player, but in terms of quality it has a wholly enviable reputation.

The first grapevines were planted in 1788 in Governor Phillip's garden at Farm Cove on the site of the Intercontinental Hotel in Macquarie Street, Sydney. The humid climate and summer rain soon drove the vines inland, with plantings at Parramatta, Castle Hill, Penrith and Camden flourishing by the time the first vineyard was established in the Hunter Valley in 1825.

Wine: a natural, healthy food of great antiquity

History: a bird's-eye view

The history of wine in Australia

Olive Farm houses Australia's oldest wine cellar, built in 1824.

Nineteenth century production

You may be surprised to learn that Tasmania was the second State to commence viticulture in 1823, and that it can claim to have founded both the Victorian (1834) and South Australian (1837) wine industries, as the pioneers in those two States obtained their grapevine cuttings from Tasmania. Yet they lagged behind Western Australia, thanks to the arrival of botanist Thomas Waters in 1829 with grapevines which he planted that year. In 1830 he dug the foundations of what is today Olive Farm, the oldest winery still in use in Australia, and was in commercial production by 1834.

The chart below shows the fluctuating fortunes of the States in the nineteenth century. In the closing decades Victoria was the dominant force, earning for itself the nickname John Bull's Vineyard — for much of the production was exported to the United Kingdom. However, the combined effects of phylloxera (the minute parasite which attacks the roots of the vine) which devastated Victoria but which was kept out of South Australia, the removal of State trade barriers and duties in the wake of Federation, and the move away from table wine to fortified wine production saw South Australia move to the position of dominance it retains to this day.

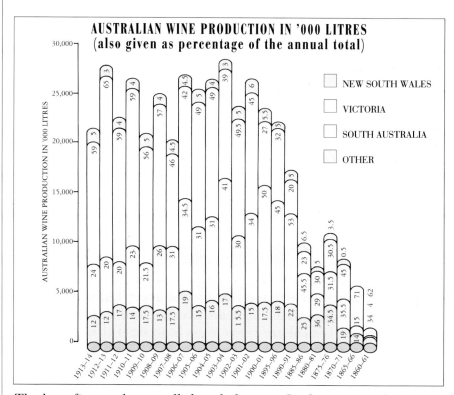

The changing viticultural map

The bare figures do not tell the whole story. In the nineteenth century grapes were grown across the length and breadth of Victoria, in particular following the footsteps of the gold miners after 1851. The Yarra Valley and Geelong were extremely important wine-producing areas, with a reputation for quality second to none. Yet not only in Victoria but right across Australia grapes were grown in regions which lapsed into obscurity for seventy years or more: when in the sixties, seventies and eighties vineyards were planted in 'new' areas, a little research soon turned up a rich viticultural history. So after a period of

geographical contraction to the heartlands of the Barossa and Hunter Valleys and of the Riverlands, the map is once again expanding to take on its nineteenth century shape, and providing an immense diversity of wine styles to choose from.

The quality of Australian wine

Curiously, although perhaps consistently with our tendency to belittle ourselves, Australians are reluctant to acknowledge just how good our wine is in world terms. If, however, you look at the books written by the leading British wine writers, or at the major English wine magazines — or even at the principal American wine magazines — another perspective emerges. Our Chardonnays and Cabernet Sauvignons (to take but two examples) are rated among the best in the world, bowing only to the finest wines of France. Another litmus test awaits the traveller overseas who casually buys wine in restaurants or shops: particularly in mainland Europe, a dreadful shock is at hand. Wine tends to be very expensive and not very good, or less expensive and quite appallingly bad.

Why is Australian wine so good?

Why, then, is Australian wine so good? Well, we have a number of advantages. First, and most obviously, there is our climate, blessed with sunshine and warmth. Indeed contrary to Europe, the limitation on viticulture is not too little warmth, but too much. Chateau Hornsby at Alice Springs proves all things are possible, but little more than that. So it is that viticulture tends to be concentrated in the south-eastern quarter of Australia, with outposts in Western Australia and Queensland. In this quarter, vines flourish, and suitable land is available on a scale undreamt of in Europe. We are able to consistently produce high yields of disease-free grapes to provide an economical and reliable raw material base for our wineries.

Research and technology

If you are ready to believe we are a nation of farmers, it may come as a surprise to find that for much of this century Australia has been in the vanguard of worldwide viticultural and oenological research. The benefits of this research have been methodically utilised in the real world of commercial winemaking, supporting a high degree of technical sophistication in our wineries.

RIGHT: Glassware of the kind found in most winery laboratories and used to determine sulphur dioxide levels.

For if our warm summer temperatures are conducive to ripening healthy grapes, the heat poses real problems for winemaking. Australia has overcome this by extensive use of refrigeration, by mechanical harvesting of grapes at night, and by extreme care in handling the grape juice and thereafter the young wine until it is bottled.

Australian wine: user-friendly

Finally, and most importantly, the wine markets of the world have pronounced their verdict: the style of Australian wine is precisely in tune with what the market wants. In a word, our wines are user-friendly. They are soft, they are fruity, they have plenty of flavour, they are clean (both in terms of flavour and in terms of additions or contaminants), and they can be enjoyed while young. Which is just as well, because over 90 per cent of all wine is consumed within days of purchase.

A Joseph's Coat: every kind of wine

As I explain later in this book, Australia makes virtually every kind of wine to be found elsewhere in the world. We produce sherry second only to Spain; vintage and tawny port second only to Portugal (though South Africa might dissent); we make sweet Riesling table wine of a quality which makes the Germans nervous; and of course our dry white and red table wines draw their inspiration from the three greatest wine-growing regions of France — Bordeaux (where Cabernet Sauvignon and Merlot grapes reign supreme), Burgundy (Chardonnay and Pinot Noir grapes) and the Rhône Valley (the Shiraz or, as we sometimes call it, the Hermitage, grape). As if all this were not enough, we are also making increasingly superb sparkling wine, and finally have our utterly unique wines, the fortified wines of North-east Victoria, which we call muscat and tokay.

ABOVE: An ancient muscat, so thick and concentrated it paints the sides of the glass.

I will take you through the most important grapes and the most important wine styles, describe how they are made, and will endeavour to explain why they taste the way they do. But try not to be intimidated or confused by the seemingly endless list of wine names and grape varieties: start with a few wines which through experience you come to know and trust, and simply build from there. Wine is one of the greatest of God's gifts: enjoy it for what it is.

3 HOW THE VINE GROWS
THE IMPORTANCE OF CLIMATE AND SOIL

'Wine is one of the noblest cordials in nature.'
JOHN WESLEY

The grapevine is an ancient plant, coming from a family which has a much longer history than humans. The particular species we now cultivate is descended from *vitis vinifera silvestris*, which appeared around the same time as Peking Man, growing in the forests (hence *sylvestris*) which covered much of the earth at the time.

It is this forest ancestry — coupled with the fact that the plant is a vine — which is responsible for the way the grapevine grows and the way it responds to human domestication of it. Only in Italy can one still find the grapevine given free reign to climb up poplars, or up and along massive overhead pergolas, in much the same way as its ancestors. Three thousand years ago the Egyptians began to plant the vine in the neat, small rows which are the hallmark of the modern vineyard, and to develop the severe winter pruning which annually reduces the vine to a fraction of its size at the end of the preceding autumn.

In its original, wild state the grapevine can climb 20 or 30 metres in its quest for the sunlight which is one of the three essentials for its continued growth and reproduction. Sunlight is the trigger for photosynthesis, the mechanism which causes all plants to grow. If the vine grows less quickly than its competitor plants, and does not reach the top of the forest where sunlight is plentiful, it cannot survive. So if it is in shade, it will divert all of its attention and available energy to one or two growing shoots (or canes) and will suppress any tendency to form grape bunches. Also, if the growing tip is cut or damaged, a hormone response will ensure that maximum growth energy is directed to the point of interruption so that the upwards fight for sunlight can be quickly resumed. Understanding this ancestry is fundamental to modern methods of vine trellising and training, to which we come in a moment.

The diagram (page 14) shows the way the vine obtains its four building blocks of water, nutrients, carbon dioxide and sunlight, a method shared by virtually all plants. The shape, the size, the quality and the quantity of these building blocks are essentially determined by the climate and the soil in which the vine is grown.

Which of climate and soil is the most important in determining the style of the world's great wines is a difficult question. I shall start with climate, simply because it is the most complex and ultimately the most important in determining whether or not grapes can be successfully grown (which is a quite different issue to that of style).

An ancient history

BELOW: Neatly trimmed vine rows at Coldstream Hills.

The quest for sunlight

HOW DOES THE VINE GROW?

CLIMATE

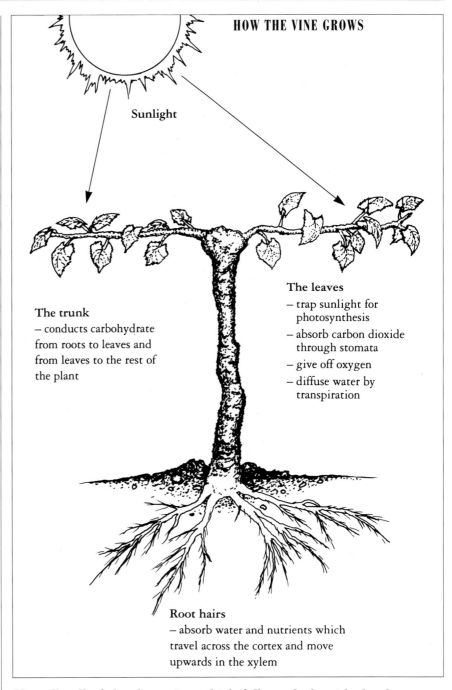

HOW THE VINE GROWS

Sunlight

The trunk
– conducts carbohydrate from roots to leaves and from leaves to the rest of the plant

The leaves
– trap sunlight for photosynthesis
– absorb carbon dioxide through stomata
– give off oxygen
– diffuse water by transpiration

Root hairs
– absorb water and nutrients which travel across the cortex and move upwards in the xylem

Winter dormancy

Virtually all of the discussion which follows deals with the dormancy needs of the vine in its seven-month active growing season. Its requirements during its winter dormancy are minimal, and are invariably satisfied in Australasia. Only in the northern United States, China and occasionally in Europe does winter have much influence: *vitis vinifera* is liable to damage if winter frosts take the temperature below -15 degrees Celsius (5 degrees Fahrenheit), and can indeed be killed outright if the temperature falls low enough, as it did in the French winter of 1956. Short of such low temperatures, deep dormancy brought on by zero or subzero winter temperatures is highly desirable: the cold kills many vine pests (mildew spores, mites and so forth) which hibernate in the bark, and promotes a more even budburst the following spring.

LEFT: *The first days of budburst; in a few weeks this bud will be a shoot half a metre long.*

Spring budburst

The initial burst of growth in spring is prompted as much by the rise in the temperature of the soil as by air temperature. It is fuelled not by photosynthesis, but by the stored reserves of carbohydrate in the roots, trunk and canes of the vine. It works like a push start for a car with a flat battery: once the leaves unfurl in sufficient quantity the photosynthetic production of fresh carbohydrate can commence and sustain the almost riotous growth which follows.

Sunlight and temperature

Astute readers may have already realised there is no necessary link between sunlight and temperature; and indeed the temperature requirements of the vine are more stringent and restrictive than they are for sunlight. The vine will not grow at mean temperatures below 10 degrees Celsius (50 degrees Fahrenheit); its optimum growth is at average temperatures falling between 15 degrees Celsius and 25 degrees Celsius (59 and 77 degrees Fahrenheit); and as the mean temperature rises above 25 degrees Celsius, the growth rate slows down. Put briefly, a vine can have too little warmth or too much, but it cannot have too much sunlight. (Incidentally, while the clarity of the sunlight — or the amount of cloud — has some significance, you can treat sunlight as meaning daylight.)

Rainfall and humidity

The next thing a vine needs for growth is an adequate supply of moisture in the ground. Just how much the vine will need is, however, dependent on the temperature and the relative humidity. The higher the temperature and the lower the relative humidity, the more the vine will transpire (or sweat) water through its leaves. Because of these variables it is not feasible to say exactly how much rainfall a vine needs in the growing season; in any event, much will depend on the moisture-holding qualities of the soil and subsoil. For all that, the table (on pages 16–17) gives the climatic data for Australasian regions.

CLIMATE
A Comparison of Regions in Australasia

STATION	REGION	MJT[1] (°C)	MAR[2] (°C)	HDD[3] (°C)	Annual RAIN (mm)	Oct-Apr Month RAIN (mm)	ARIDITY[4] (mm)	RH[5] per cent	SSH[6] hours per day
VERY HOT >23.0°C									
Alice Springs	Central Australia	29.4	17.5	337.0	250	170	810	31	10
Roma	Queensland	27.3	15.2	3140	600	400	240	56	9.0
Swan Upper	Swan Valley	24.3	11.4	2340	740	145	530	47	9.7
Mildura	Sunraysia	23.9	13.7	2240	280	130	640	49	9.7
Griffith	Murrumbidgee Irrigation Area	23.8	15.3	2201	410	200	510	51	9.3
Swan Hill	Central Murray	23.6	14.3	2150	350	150	500	52	(9.3)
Cowra	Lachlan Valley	23.5	15.5	2070	660	370	(330)	51	(9.0)
Loxton	Riverland	23.0	13.2	2080	270	130	510	51	9.6
Roseworthy	Adelaide Plains	23.0	13.2	2081	270	130	510	51	9.6
HOT 21.0 – 22.9°C									
Mudgee	Mudgee	22.9	15.0	2050	670	360	300	63	8.0
Cessnock	Lower Hunter	22.7	12.8	2070	740	530	[50]	58	7.3
Wauchope	Hastings Valley	22.5	10.5	2310	1280	1080	[430]	67	(7.5)
Muswellbrook	Upper Hunter	22.3	12.7	2170	620	400	90	75	(7.5)
Rutherglen	North-east Victoria	22.3	15.4	1770	590	260	380	50	9.3
Clare	Clare Valley	21.9	13.6	1770	630	200	430	47	(8.8)
Southern Adelaide	Southern Vales	21.7	10.8	1910	660	180	420	49	(8.6)
Nuriootpa	Barossa Valley	21.4	12.6	1710	500	160	460	47	8.8
Seymour	Goulburn Valley	21.2	13.7	1680	600	250	310	52	9.0
WARM 20.9°C – 19°C									
Avoca	Pyrenees	20.9	13.7	1530	540	220	—	57	—
Applethorpe	Granite Belt	20.5	13.1	1703	800	500	10	69	(8.1)
Margaret River	Margaret River	20.4	7.6	1690	1160	200	(400)	62	8.1
Mount Barker	Lower Great Southern	20.4	9.8	1620	750	230	350	61	(7.9)
Padthaway	Padthaway	20.4	11.4	1610	530	180	480	65	(8.2)
Stawell	Great Western	20.2	12.2	1460	590	240	(360)	59	8.3
Canberra	Canberra	20.2	14.9	1410	630	360	—	57	—

WARM 20.9°C – 19°C continued

Milang	Langhorne Creek	19.9	10.3	1520	410	140	440	60	8.3
Mornington	Mornington Peninsula	19.9	9.8	1570	740	320	—	64	—
Coonawarra	Coonawarra	19.6	9.8	1430	650	220	350	(65)	7.8
Healesville	Yarra Valley	19.4	11.0	1490	910	400	50	63	7.4
Stirling	Adelaide Hills	19.1	11.3	1270	1120	310	—	53	(8.5)
Geelong	Geelong	19.0	9.6	1470	540	250	270	62	7.8

COOL 17.0 – 18.9°C

Napier	Hawke's Bay	18.8	10.2	1460	780	340	160	64	7.4
Gisborne	Gisborne	18.6	9.4	1380	1030	420	120	64	7.3
Kyneton	Macedon	18.5	12.5	1030	750	290	170	64	(8.0)
Ballarat	Ballarat	18.5	11.9	1110	720	310	—	59	—
Auckland	Auckland	18.1	8.2	1350	1370	560	60	72	6.6
Heywood	Drumborg	17.7	8.4	1300	850	300	—	67	7.0
Blenheim	Marlborough	17.7	11.0	1152	740	300	160	63	7.8
Launceston	Tamar Valley	17.2	10.3	1020	790	310	220	65	7.3
Nelson	Nelson	17.0	10.6	997	1000	460	80	68	7.6

COLD 16.9°C

South Hobart	South Tasmania	16.8	9.0	1000	570	280	—	56	—
Canterbury/ Christchurch	Canterbury	16.4	10.9	910	660	280	170	68	6.4

( ) denotes estimate
[ ] denotes surplus of rainfall over vineyard water requirements.

Footnotes
1. Mean January temperature.
2. Mean annual range.
3. Heat degree days (calculated by taking the difference between 10°C and the mean temperature of the month, multiplying that difference by the number of days in the month, and then adding the resultant figures for each of the seven months of the growing season).
4. The difference between rainfall and 50 per cent evaporation.
5. Humidity.
6. Mean sunshine hours per day in the growing season.

Sources of Data
(1) 'The Grape-growing Regions of Australia', Peter Dry and Richard Smart. In B. Coombe and P. Dry (eds), 'Viticulture', *Resources in Australia* Vol. 1, Australian Industrial Publishers, Adelaide (1988), pages 37–60.
(2) 'A Climatic Classification for Australian Viticultural Regions', by Richard Smart and Peter Dry, in *Australian Grapevines and Winemakers* (April 1980), pages 8–16.
(3) *Climatic Averages of Australia*, Australian Government Publishing Service, Canberra (1975).
(4) *Climate Change and the New Zealand Wine Industry — Prospects for the Third Millennium*, Richard Smart.
(5) *Summaries of Climatological Observations to 1970*, Government Printer, Wellington (1973).

The wild card is irrigation. The majority of Australian vineyards are irrigated, a practice which the French heartily disapprove of. This attitude, and the historical lack of irrigation, has led to the view that irrigation is somehow evil, and that it is at the very least inconsistent with quality. If anything, the reverse is the case: to produce quality fruit, a vine must be in balance, and the stress associated with insufficient moisture is wholly harmful. The French attitude is no more or less a reflection of the fact that summer/autumn rainfall is plentiful in that country. Like all things in life, moderation is the key: if excess water is poured on to pump up the crop, or if other conditions are unfavourable (poor soil, too much heat and so forth) quality will suffer accordingly.

Just as humans suffer from the wind chill factor, so do vines. Modern research has highlighted just how much wind can impede the ripening process, quite apart from the physical damage of extreme weather conditions. Even moderate wind causes the 'breathing' action involved in photosynthesis to slow, ultimately causing a complete shut down in the system.

There are wide-ranging opinions on the importance of soil. One extreme view is that the principal function of soil is simply to provide anchorage, a solid medium in which the vine's roots can grow and thereby support the productive part of the vine (which is above ground). In other words, water and nutrients can be supplied independently — either through the irrigation system or (theoretically) via a full-blown hydroponics system.

At the other end of the spectrum is the view of the French, who regard soil as all-important. They in fact use the term *terroir* which one distinguished French vigneron has described as 'the coming together of the climate, the soil and the landscape. It is the combination of an infinite number of factors: temperatures by night and by day, rainfall distribution, hours of sunlight, soil acidity, presence of minerals, depth, water-retention, exposure to sunlight, slope and drainage to name but a few. All these factors react with each other to form, in each part of the vineyard, what French wine growers call a terroir.'

It follows that each terroir is unique and unrepeatable, and makes sense of vineyard land values of up to $2.5 million per hectare. It is why the French are able to say one can grow and make Chardonnay anywhere, but one can only make White Burgundy in Burgundy (and coincidentally, as it were, use the Chardonnay grape variety to do so).

The more extreme 'terroirists' allege a direct link between the mineralogical and (possibly) organic nutrient content of the soil and grape flavour. It leads to the suggestion that certain grape varieties need certain specific types of soil (such as limestone), without which quality will suffer. While strongly held, the view is without scientific proof.

The better view is that the structure of the soil is what is most important. It should promote the growth of the vine's roots both near the surface and at depth; it should be free-draining yet at the same

Irrigation: a dirty word

OPPOSITE: Spray irrigation is often used in preference to drip irrigation which is more expensive. Drip irrigation is used where water is scarce or disease a problem.

Wind

SOIL

The French view

ABOVE: Sandy alluvial soils promote vine growth and high crop levels.

Soil and grape flavour: linked or not

Soil structure

RIGHT: *The celebrated red soil and infamous black soil of Coonawarra.*

time have the capacity to store moisture for release over a prolonged period of time; and it should have the capacity to absorb and store daytime heat and re-radiate it during the night.

Soil types

In practical terms three soil types satisfy these requirements: gravelly alluvials, limestone-based or impregnated soils, and permeable clay loams. In all three cases the presence of rocks and stones is crucial, aiding drainage and root penetration, and acting as efficient heat storage and re-radiation centres. Soils which are less suitable are heavy clays, thin, sandy soils, and rich alluvials. One can find vineyards on such soils, but not vines capable of producing real quality.

MODERN CANOPY CONTROL

In the past decade a great deal of practical research has gone into various methods of training and shaping the vine's canopy— that profusion of new canes, leaves and ultimately grape bunches which form in each growing season. This research can more easily be understood if you remember the ancestry of the vine which I explained at the start of this chapter.

Essentially, the aim is to create a vine with the correct balance between the amount of canes, leaves and bunches, and in which the optimum amount of sunlight penetrates the canopy and falls on those bunches.

To prune or not to prune

Since the time of the Egyptians and until very recently, this has been achieved by annual winter pruning, and what is more, by pruning very severely. Because the vine has no surrounding competition, and is usually given a trellis to grow along, the system works well where the combination of soil (or terroir), climate, planting density (the number of vines per hectare (acre)) and pruning method leads to a balanced vine with appropriate sunlight penetration. The thrust of recent research has been to improve that balance and sunlight penetration, partly by new trellis designs, partly by mechanised winter pruning, and partly by summer trimming and leaf removal around the grape bunches (the so-called fruiting zone).

Australia has, however, developed an entirely different approach, which is essentially no pruning at all, even though it is euphemistically called minimal pruning. The vine is left to grow unchecked, with heavy reliance on a hitherto unsuspected ability to self regulate that growth and to produce bunches on the outside of the canopy where maximum sunlight will reach the grapes. Yields typically increase, with far more bunches of smaller than usual size. Those who use the system say quality is improved, those who oppose it say quality suffers: all agree it eliminates one of the most costly components of viticulture, which is pruning.

This leads directly to the most contentious issue of all: what is the optimum level of production, or yield. It is an exceedingly complex subject, and whatever answer one gives has to be hedged with all sorts of qualifications. With the benefit of 1000 years (give or take a bit) of experience, the French have come up with a figure of 6.8 tonnes per hectare (2.7 tonnes per acre) (which they express as 45 hectolitres per hectare, meaning 4500 litres (1000 gallons) of must — or crushed grapes and juice — per hectare).

This figure, however, takes no account of the planting density; many argue it is the yield per vine which matters. Others take the argument further, suggesting it is the yield per centimetre of fruit-bearing wood which should be calculated; others prefer to talk in terms of buds per hectare.

Australian solution: minimal pruning

YIELD AND QUALITY

BELOW: The vines on the left have been minimally pruned; those on the right mechanically pruned by tractor-mounted cutter bars.

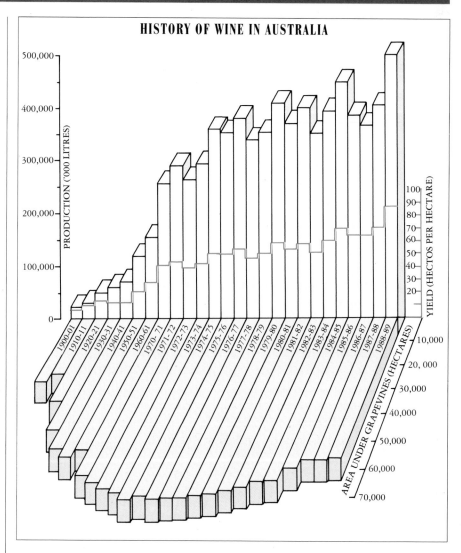

HISTORY OF WINE IN AUSTRALIA

What is clear is that at some point, the quality of the grapes starts to diminish as the yield increases. That point is reached earlier (that is at lower yields) with red wines than white wines. I personally believe the figure to be around 7.5 tonnes per hectare (3 tonnes per acre) for red wines, and 11.5 tonnes per hectare (4.5 tonnes per acre) for whites. However, there is a certain degree of elasticity, and quality may not diminish significantly until those figures are exceeded by more than 50 per cent.

As the chart (above) shows, yields in Australia have risen dramatically since the turn of the century, and are now well above my postulated limits. Bear in mind, too, these are average yields: the actual yields in some regions — particularly the Riverlands — are much higher. But this is precisely the reason why cask wine is so cheap on the one hand, and on the other why there is a vast difference between the quality of a top Cabernet Sauvignon in a bottle and that of a Cabernet Sauvignon cask.

4 GRAPE VARIETIES

'Grudge myself good wine? As soon as grudge my horse corn.' WILLIAM THACKERAY

Introduction: vitis vinifera

There are more than 1000 different grape varieties used for wine-making. Many are varieties, or cultivars, of *vitis vinifera*; these are descendants of a single vine (or possibly several vines) selected from the wild thousands of years ago. The overwhelming majority of the grape varieties grown in Australia (and used for winemaking) are *vitis vinifera* varieties. Household names are Chardonnay, Semillon, Cabernet Sauvignon and Shiraz, but there are many more.

Vinifera crosses

The next group are crosses of *vitis vinifera* varieties: these are bred by cross-pollination of two different varieties, a technique pioneered by a Frenchman Louis Bouschet in 1824 and perfected by German research scientists in the second half of the nineteenth century, but also used in countries such as France, the United States and Australia. One of the best known examples is Muller Thurgau, the most widely grown grape in both Germany and New Zealand.

Hybrids

Then there are the hybrids, which are crosses between *vitis vinifera* and, typically, *vitis labrusca* varieties. Relatively few of these are grown in Australia, although they are common in some parts of the world, particularly North America and, at one time, New Zealand. Chambourcin is the principal local example of a hybrid, grown chiefly in the Hastings Valley on the mid-north coast of New South Wales.

Finally, there are the non-vinifera species (*V. labrusca, V. rotundifolia*) selected from the wild in the same way as *vitis vinifera*. Here the best-known examples are the North American species.

LEFT: This is the 100th time these Shiraz vines have produced the lime green leaves of early spring.

PRINCIPAL WINE VARIETIES

Grape Name (and alternative names) and statistics	Best Regions in Australia	Good Australian Makers	Style of Wine	Overseas Equivalent
CHARDONNAY Pinot chardonnay 1991 tonnes 38 000 1994 tonnes 67 200 (projected)	Hunter Valley NSW; Southern Victoria; Padthaway, Coonawarra, Southern Vales SA, Margaret River WA (but is grown everywhere and seldom disappoints.)	Allanmere, Evans Family, Leeuwin Estate, Moorooduc Estate, Lindemans, Mountadam, Nicholson River, Petaluma, Pierro, Plantagenet, Rosemount, Rothbury, St.Huberts, Seppelt, Tarrawarra, Thomas Hardy, Tyrrell, Wirra Wirra.	Almost always oak-influenced, usually giving a spicy or a lemony taste which ideally blends smoothly with the fruit flavour which may be reminiscent of fig, melon, peach, or grapefruit. Becomes honeyed and buttery with age. SUMMARY: dry, full bodied and rich.	Burgundy, France (which includes Chablis) is the home of the most famous (and expensive) Chardonnay, making tremendously rich, complex and long lived wines. Very successful and widely grown in United States particularly California, and it is the coming variety in countries such as Italy, Austria, Chile, South Africa and Spain.
RHINE RIESLING Riesling Johannesberg Riesling 1991 tonnes 41 500 1994 tonnes 54 400 (projected)	Clare Valley, Eden Valley, Barossa Valley, Adelaide Hills, SA; Great Southern, WA; Tasmania	Alkoomi, Capel Vale, Castle Rock, Goundrey, Heggies, Leo Buring, Mitchell, Mitchelton, Orlando, Petaluma, Pewsey Vale, Plantagenet, Seppelt, Tim Knappstein, Thomas Hardy, Wolf Blass.	Made without any oak and bottled early. The aroma is initially in the lime/citrus/passionfruit spectrum, building first a toasty character and ultimately a kerosene-like edge (not unpleasant) with age. The flavours are similar, but the taste can be dry, medium, sweet or very sweet (as to sweet Rieslings see Ch. 10). SUMMARY: crisp, fresh, aromatic and tingling, light bodied.	Germany is recognised premium producer; until recently most of the best wines were moderately to extremely sweet, and of very different style to those of Australia. The new wave dry or trocken wines are much lighter in flavour than those of Australasia. Alsace, France makes a strong, dry Riesling, much tougher than ours; the U.S.A. (California and Washington State) can make quite similar wines.
SEMILLON Hunter River Riesling 1991 tonnes 36 200 1994 tonnes 55 500 (projected)	Hunter Valley, Mudgee, Griffith, NSW; Barossa Valley, SA; Margaret River, WA.	Allanmere, Basedows, Brokenwood, Evans & Tate, Lindemans, McWilliams, Mosswood, Rosemount, Rothbury, Tyrrells, Willespie; also de Bortoli, Peter Lehmann, Wilton Estate (these three for botrytis styles).	Made in three distinct manifestations: dry, unwooded requiring many years of bottle age to reach its best; dry but oaked, which can be consumed while much younger; and thirdly as a lusciously sweet dessert style, heavily influenced by botrytis. When young, the classic dry non-oaked wine is thin and faintly grassy (unless it be from the Margaret River in which case it is very grassy) needing years in bottle to build flavour and texture. SUMMARY: very versatile, light to full-bodied.	The only direct equivalent is of the third style, provided by French Sauternes. Australia is the only country to produce significant quantities of high quality dry white wine from the grape.

SAUVIGNON BLANC Fume Blanc 1991 tonnes 8600 1994 tonnes 14 600 (projected)	Southern Vales, Coonawarra, SA; Margaret River, WA.	Cape Mentelle, Evans & Tate, Hill Smith Estate, Katnook, Leeuwin Estate, Saltram, Shaw & Smith, Stafford Ridge, Wirra Wirra.	Again a chameleon, particularly if fume blanc is regarded as a variant of sauvignon blanc (legally there is no connection between the two). Is made in both oaked and unoaked versions, the latter crisp, pungent and redolent of gooseberries at their best. By and large the wines do not benefit from cellaring. SUMMARY: trendy, and best young, crisp and fruity.	The Loire Valley, France is the home of Sancerre and Pouilly fume, generally regarded as the yardsticks for the rest of the world. California does well with the variety, while it is an important component (along with Semillon and Muscadelle) in both dry and sweet wines from Bordeaux (including sauternes).
CABERNET SAUVIGNON Cabernet 1991 tonnes 32 400 1994 tonnes 45 800 (projected)	Coonawarra, Clare Valley, Barossa Valley, Langhorne Creek, Southern Vales, SA; Bendigo, Yarra Valley, Vic; Mudgee, NSW; Margaret River, Great Southern, WA.	Bowen Estate, Cape Mentelle, Cullens, Goundrey, Henschke, Hollick, Leeuwin Estate, Lindemans, Mildara, Mount Mary, Mosswood, Orlando, Penfolds, Petaluma, Wynns, Yarra Yering.	Varies significantly according to the climate in which the grapes are grown, more chocolatey and rich in warmer regions, more austere in cooler areas, but always with blackcurrant, raspberry and sometimes mulberry fruit flavour augmented by tannin and (particularly in the best wines) a touch of spicy or vanillan oak. The wines are all long-lived, improving for up to 20 years in bottle. SUMMARY: full bodied, strongly structured and long-lived.	Bordeaux, France, makes the cabernet-based wines; in the Haut Medoc and Graves sub-districts Cabernet is the most important grape, but is blended with smaller percentages of Merlot, Cabernet Franc, Malbec and Petit Verdot. Likewise the dominant red variety in California, but of ever increasing importance in the world e.g. Bulgaria, Russia, Italy, Chile, South Africa.
SHIRAZ Hermitage 1991 tonnes 54 800 1994 tonnes 66 100 (projected)	Hunter Valley, NSW; Coonawarra, Barossa Clare Valley, Southern Vales, SA; Great Western, Macedon, Vic.	Bests, Brokenwood, Chateau Tahbilk, Draytons, Henschke, Knights, Lindemans, Mount Langi Ghiran, Penfolds, St. Hallett, Seppelt, Wendouree, Wynns, Yarra Yering.	There are four styles of shiraz: the pepper/spice Rhone Valley look-alikes of Central and Southern Victoria; the lush, concentrated and dense wines of the Barossa Valley, exemplified by Grange Hermitage; the smooth, red cherry and mint style of Coonawarra, Clare and parts of Central Victoria; and the earthy, velvety reds of the Hunter Valley. Like Cabernet Sauvignon, the best wines benefit from prolonged cellar age. SUMMARY: multi-faceted, medium to full-bodied, long-lived – and underrated.	The northern Rhone Valley (particularly Cote Rohe and Hermitage) produces superlative wine from 100% shiraz. As one moves south, other grapes are used in blends to make wines of not dissimilar style. But as with Semillon, Australia is the only other country to make significant quantities of high quality Shiraz.

| PINOT NOIR
Pinot

1991 tonnes 8400
1994 tonnes 13 400
(projected) | Yarra Valley, Geelong, Mornington Peninsula, Macedon, Gippsland, Vic; Adelaide Hills, SA; Lower Great Southern, WA; Tasmania. | Bannockburn, Bass Philip, Coldstream Hills, de Bortoli, Diamond Valley, Dromana Estate, Mount Mary, Mountadam, Kings Creek, St. Huberts, Wignalls. | Pinot Noir should be highly aromatic and intense in flavour, with a long finish, yet retain an almost flowery delicacy. Because it is low in tannin and light in colour and total extract, it is lightbodied, and for all of these reasons cannot be compared to any other red wine. While there are exceptions, most Pinots are at their best within five years of vintage. SUMMARY: intensely fragrant and silky fruit. | Burgundy, France is the ancestral home of Pinot Noir, and is universally regarded as making its finest wine, albeit in small quantities, making the wine both scarce and expensive. Elsewhere it has proved difficult to grow and make: the Central Coast of California, Oregon, Martinborough (New Zealand), and the 'dress circle' around Melbourne are the few outstanding regions in the world. |

RIGHT: The pink seeds of as-yet translucent Chardonnay grapes; it will be many weeks before this bunch will be ready for harvest.

Most of the hybrids and all of the American species have a very particular and not-terribly pleasant taste, usually described as foxy. Concord, a variety of *vitis labrusca* is the most famous (or infamous) of the native grapes; Niagara is an equally foxy cross between Concord and Cassady (another American variety); while most of the *labrusca-vinifera* crosses are almost equally unpleasant.

American hybrids — a particular 'foxy' taste

Why, then, are hybrids and American species used in the first place? Basically, to produce a vine which performs better in the particular climate in which it is grown. The American species and the hybrids are resistant to mildews, and can be more easily grown in wet, warm and humid climates. They may be more resistant to other diseases, and likewise to extreme winter frosts.

Why hybrids?

Their drawback is, of course, that the taste is considered by connoisseurs to be less attractive than that of *vitis vinifera*. Even *vinifera* crosses are yet to produce a wine of quality superior to the traditional (native) varieties, but the search goes on. The successes have been varieties which have some specific redeeming feature or characteristic: increased yield, earlier ripening, better colour or so forth — but not better flavour.

So it is that all of the major grape varieties used in Australia are *vitis vinifera* cultivars descended from the wild. Not, of course, that there are any grapevines native to Australia: they were all imported, many by the early settlers. The two most significant importations were by William Macarthur in 1817 and by James Busby in 1833 (both to Sydney), although the other States also brought in vines direct. While many of the varieties brought in by Busby and Macarthur were 'lost' in the sense that their true identity was forgotten and local or incorrect names were given to them, isolated plantings survived and were rediscovered (or correctly identified) in the years after the Second World War, thanks both to French experts and to the late Allan Antcliff of the CSIRO.

The first vines in Australia

A final word of explanation on what is a fairly complex subject. Each grape variety has a number of clones. A clone is a member of a group of plants (in the case of vines) propagated asexually from a single source. Traditionally this was done by taking cuttings, however, it is now also achieved through in vitro cell propagation.

Clones

Different clones have different characteristics. Some yield better, some have better colour, some have more flavour, some less. Particularly since 1960 there have been special importations of clones, principally from California, but more recently France, aimed at increasing the choice for winemakers. For various reasons, most to do with plant health and disease, the inflow of new clones has been severely restricted, and the future improvement of grape and wine quality is closely tied up with greater access and choice.

We shall now turn to the main grape varieties grown in Australia. Like so many others, the most important white variety — Chardonnay — has been here since the earliest days, when it was often called White Pineau. However, it gradually disappeared from view, and when

WHITE GRAPE VARIETIES
CHARDONNAY

Murray Tyrrell released Vat 47 Chardonnay in 1971, it was the first wine this century to be marketed under its true name. (Well, not quite: Tyrrell called it Pinot Chardonnay, which is technically incorrect.)

The wine won instant acclaim, ensuring both for itself and the Hunter Valley as a whole, a tasting reputation for premium quality. Because of quarantine laws in South Australia designed to prevent a tiny but devastating parasite called phylloxera ever entering the State, and lack of initial interest in Victoria, New South Wales had a ten year start on the field. The explosion in production has really been a phenomenon of the second half of the 1980s, continuing on to the 1990s.

It is a tremendously flexible and adaptable variety, adjusting itself to a wide range of climate and soil. It is equally easy to work with in the winery, presenting the winemaker with many choices in shaping the style of wine he or she wishes to make — something we will look at further in Chapter 9. So far as you are concerned, Chardonnay is one of the easiest wines to enjoy: it is friendly, soft and always flavoursome. If it has a drawback for the beginner, it may be that it has too much flavour, too much richness, but you should find that to be a passing phase.

RIESLING

Until the arrival of Chardonnay, Rhine Riesling was the most important high quality grape, although the extent of that importance was partially obscured by the misuse of the word Riesling. On the one hand, there was Hunter River Riesling (in fact Semillon) and Clare Valley Riesling (in fact Crouchen, a distinctly inferior variety); on the other hand, Riesling was widely used not so much as the name of a grape variety but simply to denote a wine style, in the same way as hock, chablis, white burgundy and so forth. Hock is used no more, and the word Riesling to indicate style is diminishing, being used mainly on wine casks.

True Riesling (and that, incidentally, is its correct name, without 'Rhine') has always had its stronghold in South Australia, and in particular in the Barossa, Eden and Clare Valleys. It also performs quite brilliantly in the Lower Great Southern region of Western Australia, making long-lived wines of great elegance. Only New South Wales seems unsuited to the grape.

From a high point of popularity and demand in the late seventies, demand for Rhine Riesling plummeted in the early eighties, but has steadily recovered since that time. Partly because it is rarely given any oak maturation or oak flavour, and partly because of the variety, the wine is crisp, clean and delicate in flavour. If a little sweetness is left in the wine, it is an ideal entry point for you to start serious drinking as you graduate from casks. What is more, it always offers excellent value for money; even the best Rhine Rieslings are, relatively speaking, cheap.

SEMILLON

Next in importance is Semillon, a variety which formed a unique bond with the Hunter Valley going back to the mid-nineteenth century when it was called Shepherd's Riesling. Its dominance in the Hunter Valley lasted 150 years; only in the past few years has Chardonnay overtaken it in terms of plantings, and in any event the experts would argue that Semillon produces greater wine in the Hunter than does Chardonnay, particularly if it is aged for ten or twenty years in bottle. Just why the climate and soils of the Hunter Valley are so suited to Semillon is not known, and certainly cannot be explained by the infinitely cooler climate of Bordeaux, the only other district in which it produces wine of such exceptional quality (though very different style). Its other regions include Mudgee, Margaret River, the Barossa Valley and (for sweet white table wine) the Griffith district. The wine comes in many guises. When it is young and unoaked it is dry, faintly grassy and relatively low in flavour; if you like subtle tastes, or are looking for a simple cool drink for a summer's day, Semillon may be the answer. With oak flavour, or with age, the wine becomes richer, nuttier and more honeyed, tasting much more like a Chardonnay.

We now step down a notch in importance: the remaining white grapes are either grown in lesser quantities or are statistically important but are considered to make wine of lesser quality.

SAUVIGNON BLANC

Sauvignon Blanc is an even more recent arrival on the scene than is Chardonnay. It tends to sharply polarise opinions between judges: you either enjoy the tart, green gooseberry aroma and flavour or you perceive the taste as being akin to cat's pee. That dilemma, I should hasten to add, exists only with good Sauvignon Blanc; much of lesser quality from warmer parts of Australia doesn't taste of anything much at all, and is frequently blended with Semillon, Chenin Blanc or anything else which comes readily to hand. That blend, ironically, is particularly common in the Margaret River region where it is often called Margaret River Classic or Classic Dry White: ironically, because this is one of the areas in which the variety does well. As each year goes by, grape growers are growing better Sauvignon Blanc with more varietal flavour, and winery techniques are responding, but New Zealand still has a comfortable edge over Australia.

CHENIN BLANC

If you are looking for a wine with soft, slightly bland flavour — in which no one taste seems to stand out — Chenin Blanc may be the grape for you. It is grown everywhere and achieves real distinction nowhere; its main virtue is relatively high yields which make it a useful 'filler' in blended wines sold as Chablis, White Burgundy, etc.

COLOMBARD

Colombard fulfils much the same role, but does it rather better. Its great advantage is its ability to retain relatively high levels of natural acidity in warm regions, an ability which has seen plantings increase from zero in the early seventies to the point where it ranks in the top half dozen premium white varieties. Only a few makers release a varietal Colombard — Primo Estate in the Adelaide Plains is an outstanding example — with most being used in so-called Chablis.

TRAMINER

Traminer or Gewurztraminer (two names for precisely the same grape) had a brief period of extreme popularity in the late sixties and early seventies, but still remains one of the best grapes of all for the beginner to cut his or her teeth on.

As you become more confident with wine, and get to the stage where you consciously seek to identify the grape variety by smell and taste (rather than reading the label), it is long odds on your first success will come with Traminer. You can actually smell and taste the grape in the wine, almost as if it had not been fermented; alternatively, think of a fresh lychee with a little added spice.

Penfolds (with a wine they no longer make called Bin 202) and Wyndham Estate with Bin TR222 blended Traminer with Rhine Riesling, and left a little sweetness in the wine. It was a fantastically successful recipe, picked up much later by Wolf Blass with a Traminer Riesling blend aimed fairly and squarely at the Asian restaurant market — for it is with such food that Traminer is a great match.

MUSCAT GORDO BLANCO

Muscat Gordo Blanco (often simply called Gordo by winemakers and more correctly named Muscat of Alexandria) also has a distinctive grapey taste. Vast amounts are grown in the irrigation areas, and much finds its way into wine casks — most notably moselle — and into the cheapest sparkling wines. Its more distinguished cousin Muscat a Petits Grains, also known as Frontignac, makes intensely grapey table wine and the famous muscat fortified wine of North-east Victoria.

SULTANA, PALOMINO, DORADILLO, TREBBIANO

These varieties are included because statistically they are important, particularly the so-called multipurpose grape Sultana, used for drying, winemaking and eating fresh according to demand. You will never see these grape names on a bottle or on a cask, but it is in the latter that they end up, although Palomino can be (indeed should be) used for making sherry.

RED GRAPE VARIETIES
CABERNET SAUVIGNON

Just as Chardonnay has recently arrived on the scene to topple Rhine Riesling from its throne, so has Cabernet Sauvignon enjoyed a meteoric rise in popularity since 1960. It never quite disappeared as did Chardonnay, but the widespread plantings of the nineteenth century shrank to a few insignificant patches in South Australia and Victoria. The reason for its decline was simple enough: it was relatively low yielding (the main South Australian clone was a particularly poor one, often producing vines barren of fruit) and it was unsuited to fortified wine production.

Its rise in fortune has in turn been closely linked to the spread of grape growing from the traditional warm regions to the cooler ones — Coonawarra had less than 4 hectares (9.8 acres) planted in 1960, Padthaway none; now 859 hectares (2122 acres) are planted in those two areas. Mind you, like Chardonnay, Cabernet Sauvignon seems to do well almost wherever it is grown, even if the best examples come from the cooler climates.

Its wine always has a touch of austerity, of toughness even, and this character is more evident in cooler regions, ultimately going 'over the top' in very cold areas with an unmistakeable herbal greenness to the aroma and taste. In a perfect situation that touch of green, the hint of toughness, will be balanced by tastes of cassis (your childhood Ribena), raspberries and mulberries, the last two in moderation. Cabernet — the name is best abbreviated this way, never the loathsome 'Cab Sav' which so offends the ear of winemakers and experts — acquires a rich, dark chocolate edge in place of the green bite when grown in warmer climates, which no doubt explains why it is so popular.

Nonetheless, Cabernet still has some distance to go before it catches up with Shiraz in terms of production. Shiraz (or Hermitage as it is incorrectly called in New South Wales and by some makers elsewhere) was the backbone of the premium red wine industry for over a century. Because of this role it is to be found growing in all wine regions, remaining dominant because basically it is an easy grape to grow and provides a relatively high yield.

All grapes respond to the influence of climate, and Shiraz is no exception, producing four distinct styles. Most famous is that of the Barossa, home of Penfolds Grange Hermitage. Grange is unique, the richest, juiciest, most flavour-packed red wine imaginable, but other Shiraz wines from the South Australian districts around Adelaide share some of its fleshy, soft style, merging with some of the dark chocolate flavours to be found in Cabernet grown in similar climates.

Then there are the silky smooth, red berry wines from cooler regions, sometimes with a touch of eucalyptus mint lurking in the background. Parts of central Victoria and Coonawarra are noted for wines of this kind. We are only just starting to learn why, but these cooler regions can also produce the third style, which has a strong black pepper and spice aroma and flavour. Such wines are often lighter and a little thinner, but the best are luxuriantly textured. Finally, there are the gently earthy, faintly leathery wines made famous by the Hunter Valley, but also found in Mudgee and the Southern Vales. You may find these quite abrasive when they are young, but they undergo a transformation with age, acquiring a soft lustre like ancient polished wood; a velvety softness which is quite lovely.

Pinot Noir ranks with Cabernet Sauvignon as one of the two great red grapes of France, but nowhere else in the world has it achieved the same status. The reason is that it is a terrible traveller, being infinitely hard to please and quite impossible to second-guess in the search for climate and soil which suits it.

It is also a variety which initially you are likely to find very difficult to understand. Many indeed will go through life mystified by all the fuss about this frequently pale-coloured, frequently light-bodied wine. For a few it will become an obsession, its flowery, strawberry-plum aroma, its intense flavour, and its sheer grace making it superior to all others.

It succeeds in only a few areas in Australia, but does so in those areas in a way which most other countries outside France cannot emulate: only the central coast and southern Napa Valley of California and Oregon in the United States lay down a consistent challenge. Elsewhere in Australia it is principally used in making premium sparkling wine.

It will soon become clear to you that there are far fewer premium red grapes than there are white. Merlot ranks next, yet it has only just crept onto the statistical register, and is in any event almost always

SHIRAZ

PINOT NOIR

MERLOT

used as a junior — very junior — partner in a blend with Cabernet Sauvignon. It is usually to be found growing near Cabernet, and responds in much the same way to the influence of climate. It is distinctly softer, and even leafier than Cabernet, but blends particularly well with it.

GRENACHE AND MATARO

These two Rhône Valley varieties once totally dominated red grape plantings in Australia, but have been in free fall decline since 1970 — ironic given that the two are currently cult varieties in California with a seemingly rosy future. Of the two, Grenache is the better, and you may sometimes see the name on a bottle, particularly if it is a rosé. Otherwise, they will be consigned to the anonymity of casks or (again in the case of Grenache) used for making port of various types. Mataro, incidentally, is more correctly called Mouvedre, its French name.

5 THE WINEMAKING PROCESS

'Wine can be considered with good reason as the most healthful and the most hygienic of all beverages.'
LOUIS PASTEUR

If you should ever find your way to an amateur winemakers' wine show or exhibition you will be amazed at the range of 'wines' on display. In my early days as a wine judge I officiated at competitions offering everything from couchgrass to rose petal to rhubarb to an array of citrus-based wines. In this context the commercially available kiwifruit, apple and strawberry wines do not seem the least bit exotic.

This simply underlines the fact that almost any fruit or vegetable can be made to ferment thereby converting the sugar (or carbohydrate) present in the raw material into alcohol. The trigger for the commencement of fermentation is yeast, which is usually added in the commercial winemaking context, but which is frequently naturally present and which can lead to spontaneous fermentation, whether desired or not.

So it is with grapes: most of the greatest French wines from Bordeaux and Burgundy ferment 'naturally', that is, by relying on the wild yeasts which occur on the grape skins and which can be seen by the naked eye as a white or grey 'bloom' on the grapes. Looked at from this standpoint, the process of winemaking is as natural as it is simple: by one of nature's happiest quirks, grape skins and juice produce a biochemically safe and, if protected from oxygen, long-lived substance which we know as wine.

As I said in the introduction, modern winemaking methods do no more than ensure an appropriate degree of consistency and predictability: the winemaker has been described by some as a quality control officer, whose job is essentially to do no more than preserve what nature has given him or her. This minimalist approach to grape growing and winemaking does full justice to neither viticulturist nor winemaker, but it does help our understanding of the way wine is made.

These days most grapes are mechanically harvested by large machines which straddle the vines and partly beat, partly shake the bunches (or often just the berries) off the vine. Since 1970 the design of the harvesters has become ever more sophisticated, with specially-designed grape trellises aiding the task, and there is no longer any serious debate about loss of quality through mechanical harvesting of large vineyards. Indeed, there can be a quality gain. For one thing, harvesting is usually done at night when the grapes are much cooler, which is of particular importance for white grapes.

Almost anything will ferment

'Natural' French winemaking

The winemaker's role of quality control officer

**WINEMAKING:
THE BASIC STEPS
HARVESTING**

ABOVE: *The mechanical harvester at work.*

CRUSHING

Secondly, it allows for large areas to be picked precisely when the grapes are at their best; alternatively, if the winemaker sees an adverse weather forecast, he or she can pick immediately and avoid the weather.

The most important reason, however, is cost: one third to one quarter of that of hand picking. The latter remains the choice of makers of specialist wines requiring whole bunches (sparkling wine and pinot noir are two examples) and of the small vineyard owner. 'Hand picked' may also become a marketing tool for some super-premium wines, for in certain circumstances there can be a quality gain from hand picking even where whole bunches are not essential.

Almost all grapes are crushed when they arrive at the winery. Exceptions are sparkling wine, where the bunches may be placed directly into the press, or red wine techniques used to make beaujolais-style wines or pinot noir. The crusher does two things: it removes the berries from the stalks (the stalks being ejected from the end of the crusher) and it splits the skin of the berries. In the most modern crushers both functions are adjustable: it is possible to retain a percentage of the stalks, and to minimise the splitting or crushing of the berries.

RIGHT: *Grapes in the receival bin are fed through to the crusher by the central revolving screw.*

Red wines are fermented 'on their skins'. In other words, the porridge-like mixture of skins, pulp and juice is taken directly to the fermenter, and the skins are not removed (via the press) until the end of fermentation — or indeed some time after the end of fermentation — by which time the alcoholic conversion is complete and one has what is effectively wine.

White grapes, by contrast, are placed in the press after they have been crushed and before fermentation has commenced. The press takes many different forms: the most ancient is the basket press, the basic principles of which go back to the Middle Ages. A ratchet and vertical screw gradually force down a wooden (or nowadays metal) plate on the grape skins contained within a slotted basket, which may be round or square. At the other extreme is the horizontal bladder or membrane press, in which a rubberised bladder inside a perforated cylinder is inflated, pressing the grapes in a relatively thin layer between the bladder and the cylinder. It is a gentle and highly efficient press which extracts relatively clear juice from the skins.

In a well-equipped winery, the white grapes may well pass through a must chiller on their way from the crusher to the press, dropping the temperature by as much as 15 degrees Celsius (59 degrees Fahrenheit) (say from 25 degrees Celsius to 10 degrees Celsius (77 to 50 degrees Fahrenheit)), thereby helping reduce oxidation and reducing the need for chemical protection. (The colder the grapes, the less the need for cooling, which is one of the advantages of mechanical harvesting at night.)

The main form of chemical protection against oxidation is sulphur dioxide, and conventional winemaking will see sulphur dioxide added at the crusher for white wines, probably in tandem with ascorbic acid (which you will know as vitamin C). If the grapes are red, either no sulphur dioxide at all will be added, or only a small quantity. By the end of fermentation, whatever sulphur dioxide has been added will have disappeared altogether or become 'bound', which means it is no longer active. At some stage (or stages) before bottling, more sulphur dioxide will be added so that — typically — the wine will contain 15 to 20 parts per million (ppm) of 'free', that is, active, sulphur dioxide. This contrasts with levels of 200 ppm in fresh fruit salad or coleslaw in the health food bar.

It is this additive which gives rise to the statement 'Preservative (220) added' which you will find on almost every Australian red or white wine label. The additional statement frequently found on white wine labels 'Antioxidant (300) added' refers to the ascorbic acid, or vitamin C.

It is possible to make wine without chemical additives of any kind (using organically grown grapes for good measure). The irony is that additive-free wine is more likely to be harmful at worst, due to the fact that bacteria will grow more readily in sulphur-free wines, or simply less pleasant at best than wine made with chemical additives at the level normally encountered in Australian wine. Generally, only the

PRESSING

White grape pressing

Must chiller

CHEMICAL ADDITIVES: THE ROLE OF SULPHUR DIOXIDE

Label disclosure of additives

Organic wine

most acutely sensitive allergy- or asthma-prone person will be affected by such low levels of free sulphur dioxide, and such a person will usually be under some form of medical supervision and dietary control.

Other additives

Enzymes are sometimes added to the crushed white grapes which in effect duplicate and enhance natural processes (they aid the extraction of the juice from the skins) and will have done their work before fermentation commences, leaving no trace of their former presence in the finished wine. The other almost invariable addition is of acid, most frequently tartaric, but sometimes malic or citric. Once again, all of these acids are naturally present in lesser or greater degree; the addition is simply to redress imbalances in nature and to make the wine fresher and more enjoyable.

FERMENTATION

Wild yeasts abound in all vineyards, and fermentation will naturally commence sooner or later depending on the temperature of the must, the amount of sulphur dioxide present, and the background level of wild yeast. In fact, most Australian winemakers prefer to take out the guesswork and add cultured yeasts (isolated from wild yeasts and systematically cultured).

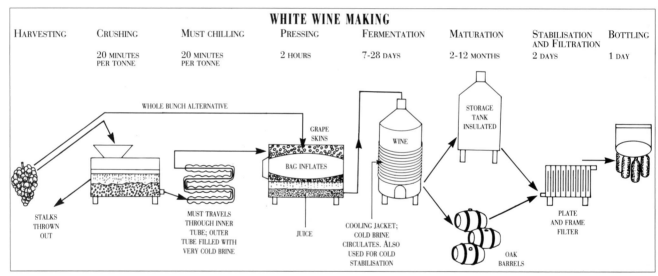

WHITE WINE MAKING

HARVESTING	CRUSHING	MUST CHILLING	PRESSING	FERMENTATION	MATURATION	STABILISATION AND FILTRATION	BOTTLING
	20 MINUTES PER TONNE	20 MINUTES PER TONNE	2 HOURS	7-28 DAYS	2-12 MONTHS	2 DAYS	1 DAY

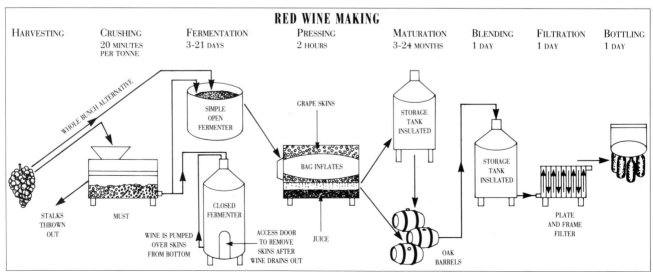

RED WINE MAKING

HARVESTING	CRUSHING	FERMENTATION	PRESSING	MATURATION	BLENDING	FILTRATION	BOTTLING
	20 MINUTES PER TONNE	3-21 DAYS	2 HOURS	3-24 MONTHS	1 DAY	1 DAY	1 DAY

What is contained in the must being fermented depends on the wine, as does the desired fermentation temperature. If it is white, only the juice (which will have been clarified by chilling, filtration or centrifugation prior to fermentation) will be in the tank or barrel, and will typically be fermented at a temperature between 10 degrees Celsius and 15 degrees Celsius (50 and 59 degrees Fahrenheit). This temperature band is significantly lower than one would expect to find in Europe, and is one of the principal reasons why Australian wines are more fruity than most of their European counterparts.

Red wines are fermented with the grape skins present, and at higher temperatures — typically 20 degrees Celsius to 28 degrees Celsius (68 to 82 degrees Fahrenheit). The presence of the skins means a different type of fermenting tank will be used to allow the agitation of the skins, which left to their own devices will rise to the top of the fermenting juice forming an ever drier and harder cap, like a pastry top on a steak and kidney pie. The type of tank and the method of mixing and agitating the skins varies greatly from wholly manual to wholly automatic, but the final aims of the agitation (often called plunging) are the same — to extract as much colour and tannin as possible from the skins, to prevent oxidation and to minimise the heat build-up which otherwise occur.

As the chart indicates, white wine fermentation is typically much longer than that of red wine, simply because the temperature is lower. But the simplified chart tells only part of the tale: while the active fermentation of the white wine extends for the full period, that of red wine is over in between three to six days. The rest of the period (if in fact used) is what is called post-fermentation maceration, designed to extract further tannins from the skins and, hopefully, soften the tannins so extracted.

If the white wine is of the aromatic type (Rhine Riesling or Traminer) or is not to be oak-influenced, it will be entirely fermented in a stainless steel tank and, as soon as fermentation is finished, will be racked off. This term describes the siphoning or pumping off of the creamy, muddy lees in the bottom of the tank which are the countless millions of dead yeast cells combined with minute pieces of particulate matter mainly deriving from grape skins. It will be filtered, cold stabilised and bottled as soon as possible — typically in June or July of the year of vintage.

If the wine is a Chardonnay, a Semillon or a Sauvignon Blanc (or any other variety to be given oak treatment) it may either be entirely fermented in small oak barrels, ideally in a cool room, or placed in barrels near the end of its primary fermentation, or it may be entirely fermented in a stainless steel tank and then, perhaps months later, placed in oak barrels. In the last decade barrel fermentation has become increasingly popular for premium white wines, even though it is more labour intensive and more difficult to control than tank fermentation. In conjunction with this trend, it has become increasingly common to leave the yeast lees in the wine, and indeed to

White wine fermentation

Red wine fermentation

ABOVE: *The beginning of fermentation producing the first bubbles of carbon dioxide.*

Length of fermentation

Aromatic or non-wooded white wines

Wooded white wines

37

RIGHT: French oak barriques.

stir these up once or twice a week for several months after the end of fermentation. The nett result is a subtly smoky aroma and a more creamy texture in the finished wine.

The wine will be racked off its lees, filtered and bottled after anything between three and fifteen months in barrel. Six to nine months is a typical sojourn for premium wine; the period is shorter for less expensive wine.

Red wine maturation

A few makers, notably Penfolds with Grange Hermitage, Wolf Blass and an increasing number of others, favour finishing red wine fermentation in barrel — the last day or half day of primary fermentation. (It is a technique which I have used in red winemaking since 1973.) Most red wine, however, is pressed long after the end of fermentation, taken to a stainless steel tank, filtered, and only then placed in barrel; this is a far simpler, more certain and less labour intensive approach. The wine will then remain in barrel for between six months and two years, with periodic intervening rackings, before being bottled.

Malolactic fermentation

At some point all red wines and some wood-matured wines undergo what is known as the malolactic fermentation, sometimes loosely called the second fermentation. This is a bacterially-triggered conversion of the naturally present malic acid in the wine to lactic acid. It produces a much softer wine, and is considered essential for reds. In many circumstances it will occur naturally, but it is increasingly common for winemakers to innoculate the wine with an appropriate bacterial culture and to carefully monitor its progress to ensure it is completed before the wine is bottled.

It is standard practice for white wines to be cold stabilised before they are bottled, although the smallest wineries may lack the equipment to achieve this. It involves chilling the wine to -2 degrees Celsius (28 degrees Fahrenheit) and holding it there for two days during which time tartrate crystals will form and drop to the bottom of the tank. If the wine is not thus stabilised, it is likely to form crystals (or what the Germans call wine diamonds) when you put the bottle into your refrigerator. These slightly milky crystals are tasteless and quite harmless, and their formation has little or no effect on the wine. But they are unsightly, and the gritty, sandy feeling in your mouth if you ingest them is far from pleasant — hence it is better to cause their formation (and to remove them) before the wine is bottled. A second form of stabilisation is also used in white wine: bentonite, a special form of clay, is added to both clarify the wine and to remove protein which may otherwise cause a milky film to appear if the wine is subjected to heat.

It is likewise standard practice for both white and red wines to be filtered before they are bottled. Because of its natural acidity (and what is called its pH) and its alcohol, wine is an extremely 'safe' substance: it will not allow pathogens harmful to humans to grow in it. But the smell and taste can be spoilt by bacterial action, and sterile filtration will prevent this occurring. Some French winemakers in particular oppose filtration, and some makers of delicate red wines such as Pinot Noir in other parts of the world do not like to use it. The argument is that it strips the wine of all or some of colour, aroma and flavour. Supporters of filtration say that provided it is properly carried out, any effect is purely temporary and that there is no scientific or objective tests which can show any adverse effect. The debate continues nonetheless.

That wine must be bottled is a self-evident truth, particularly if one treats bottling as including the filling of casks. Whether it is achieved by a modern, high-speed automated line capable of handling many thousands of bottles an hour, or whether done slowly and by hand, it requires extreme care and skill. More wine — and in particular white wine — is harmed or spoilt during bottling than at any other single stage of the winemaking process. The smaller the winery, and the less experienced the winemaker, the greater the risk — which lies chiefly in oxidation.

The wine will be stored by the winemaker for varying periods (from a few weeks to several years) before it is sold. Just as you should store wine in a cool, dark place once you have bought it (a subject I cover in detail in *Setting Up Your Own Wine Cellar* (Angus & Robertson, 1989)) so the winemaker must ensure it is stored away from heat or temperature fluctuations, ideally in an air-conditioned, insulated shed.

PACKAGING

ABOVE: A modern, high speed bottling line: the bottles have just been sterile-washed and dried.

The last link in the process of winemaking is the packaging of the wine. As you will know as soon as you walk into a well-stocked, fine wine merchant, the appearance of the bottle — the capsule, the label design, the colour and shape of the bottle — will have a major influence on the casual buyer who is not sure what he or she wants to buy when first entering the shop. The winemaker must be a person of many parts: it is not enough to know how to grow grapes and make wine, one must also be a skilled marketer.

6 TERMINOLOGY AND WINE FAULTS

*'It is a naive domestic Burgundy without any breeding,
but I think you will be amused by its presumption.'*
JAMES THURBER

This, quite frankly, is a tough chapter. It is probably best that you simply scan it briefly now, and refer back to the particular word when you come across it either elsewhere in this book or in other publications. The terminology used in relation both to winemaking and wine tasting is inevitably specialised. That of wine tasting is not only specialised but subjective and often very imprecise. It is also very easy to lampoon: James Thurber and Roald Dahl have both had a great deal of fun in attacking flowery and pretentious wine descriptions.

The difficulties of describing wine

The problem is, of course, that if you content yourself with a few basic words (light, crisp, heavy, tannic) you cannot give any idea what the wine tastes like. In the following chapter I explain how you taste wine and touch upon its actual taste; but each and every wine tastes different, so the most far-fetched terminology is to be found in individual tasting notes or wine descriptions.

Here I limit myself to the more general and commonly used terms of taste, and I have assumed there is no need to define the smell or taste of peach, pineapple, leather, linoleum or whatever reference points are used in an effort to communicate the taste of a particular wine. I shall, however, explain some technical winemaking terms, and finally some wine-fault terminology.

TASTING TERMS

First, then, tasting terms.

Aggressive

An unpleasantly obvious component of wine flavour, for example, aggressive tannin.

Aroma

The scent or smell of the grape variety; aroma decreases with age as bouquet builds.

Astringency

Sharpness or roughness deriving usually from tannin; particularly evident in a young wine, and it can be an indication of the keeping potential of such a wine.

Balance

The harmony or equilibrium between the different flavour and structure components of wine, and the first requirement of a great wine.

Big	Used to describe a wine with above-average flavour, body and/or alcohol. By no means necessarily a favourable description.
Bitter	A fault detectable at the back of the palate, usually deriving from skin, pip or stalk tannins, sometimes from mercaptan.
Body	A term used to describe the weight or substance of a wine in the mouth and deriving from alcohol and tannin. Softens and mellows with age.
Bouquet	The smell of the wine (as opposed to simply the aroma of the grape) produced by the volatile esters present in any wine. Bouquet becomes more complex during the time the wine needs to reach full maturity and finally softens and dissipates with extreme age.
Breathing	The process of allowing a wine to come in contact with air by drawing the cork (and possibly decanting) prior to serving. Enhances the development of the bouquet.
Broad	A term used to describe wine which is softly coarse, lacking in refinement.
Buttery	A term encompassing the aroma, taste and texture of a white wine, usually oak-matured, but which can also develop from long bottle-age. Typically found in Semillon and Chardonnay.
Character	The overall result of the combination of vinosity, balance and style of a wine.
Classic	A wine conforming exactly to style and of the highest quality.
Clean	The absence of any foreign (or 'off') odour or flavour; an important aspect of a wine of quality, and a term I often use.
Coarse	Indicates a wine with excessive extract of solids, particularly tannins, and probably affected by oxidation during the making process.
Complete	Denotes a wine which has all of the requisite flavours and components in harmony and balance.
Condition	A technical term to describe the clarity of a wine; a cloudy wine is described as being out of condition.
Crust	Sediment adhering to the inside of bottles of wine, usually red; consists mainly of pigment and tartrate crystals.
Developed	Showing the effects of ageing in bottle, usually but not invariably beneficially so.
Dry	A wine without apparent sweetness or residual sugar; in fact many wines contain minute traces of sugar, and it is difficult to detect at levels of up to 5 grams per litre.
Dull	Denotes a wine either cloudy or hazy in colour, or with a muted or flawed bouquet or palate.
Dumb	A wine showing either no aroma or distinct varietal taste or no development.
Earthy	Bouquet and flavour reminiscent of certain soil types; a smell of fresh earth can often be identified in young vintage port, and softer earth in old Hunter Valley dry reds.

LEFT: *David Carpenter, one half of the winemaking (and wine tasting) team at Lark Hill winery in Canberra.*

Flavourful and usually volatile substances formed by the combination of acids with alcohols. Wine probably contains over 100 different esters.	**Esters**
Soluble solids adding to the body and substance of a wine.	**Extract**
A wine past its peak, losing its bouquet, flavour and character.	**Fading**
A term denoting a wine of high quality and style, relying on subtlety rather than power for its impact.	**Finesse**
The impression a wine leaves in the mouth immediately it has been swallowed and as the first breath is taken; the aftertaste follows the finish, and is to do with flavour, whereas the finish encompasses balance, structure, texture, flavour and overall mouthfeel. The quality of the finish is of great importance in assessing wine quality.	**Finish**
A term usually applied to the finish of a wine, and denoting the impact of tannin and possibly acid.	**Firm**
A wine without sufficient acid and freshness, often due to excessive age but sometimes to poor winemaking.	**Flabby**
Similar to dull and flabby; a lack of freshness, character or acid.	**Flat**
A youthful wine with full-bodied varietal flavour, and a certain richness.	**Fleshy**
The aroma reminiscent of flowers contributed by certain aromatic grape varieties.	**Flowery**
The unpleasantly cloying, sweet aroma of wines produced from *vitis labrusca* grapes, like jujubes or boiled sweets.	**Foxy**
An aroma or taste free from any fault or bottle-developed characters, usually found in a young wine but occasionally in old wines.	**Fresh**

Fruity	The pleasant aromatic taste of a young wine with strong varietal character.
Gamy	A character reminiscent of well-hung meat or wild game which is frequently encountered in Pinot Noir or other wines made using carbonic maceration techniques, and in this context is desirable. As the aroma edges closer to that of rotten meat, it is probably a form of mercaptan, and is most undesirable.
Gassy	A wine with small bubbles of carbon dioxide, often mistaken for a form of secondary fermentation. Undesirable (particularly in red wines) but tolerated in Australia.
Generic	A wine style not linked to any particular variety, with no legal definition and which is usually borrowed (or stolen) from France, for example, chablis, burgundy, claret.
Green	Term applied to a young wine which is unbalanced because of excess malic acid deriving from unripe grapes.
Hard	An unbalanced and unyielding wine suffering, if red, from an excess of tannin and/or acid and, if white, from an excess of acid.
Harsh	Usually applied to red wine suffering from excess tannin, often when young.
Hollow	Applies to a wine with foretaste and finish, but with no flavour on the middle palate.
Honeyed	Denotes both the flavour and the structure (or feel in the mouth) of a mature white wine, particularly aged Semillon but also sauterne.
Hydrogen sulphide	The smell of rotten eggs found in red wines resulting from the reduction of sulphur dioxide or elemental sulphur. Detectable in tiny quantities (1 part per million); when bound into the wine it becomes mercaptan.
Jammy	Excessively ripe and heavy red-grape flavours, sweet but cloying.
Light	Lack of body, but otherwise pleasant.
Long	Denotes the capacity of the flavours of the wine to linger in the mouth and palate after the wine has been swallowed.
Metallic	A taste of metal, sometimes encountered in red wines which have been treated with copper sulphate to remove mercaptan.
Mousy	A peculiar flat, undesirable taste resulting from bacterial growth in wines, most evident after the wine leaves the mouth.
Mouthfeel	Literally, the overall sensation or feel of the wine in the mouth; the better and more mature the wine, the smoother, more harmonious and satisfying the feel will be. Young, full-bodied dry red wines or other immature wines tend to be uncomfortable in the mouth even if the potential is there.
Nose	The scents and odours of a wine, encompassing both aroma and bouquet.
Nutty	Characteristic pungent flavour and aroma of sherry, due in part to wood age and to the presence of acetaldehyde.

Oils deriving from grape pips or stalks and not desirable in wine.	**Oily**
May refer to a raw, harsh quality in immature wine, but increasingly recognised as a characteristic of cool climate Shiraz with pepper/spice aromas and flavones.	**Peppery**
Used to describe a faulty wine which has an excess of phenolic compounds, which are various forms of closely related chemical substances called anthocyanins, flavours and leucoanthocyanins, all of which tend to congregate in the skins and pips of the grapes. A term used mainly in relation to white wines, which have much lower levels of phenolics than do red wines but which are acutely sensitive to the presence of phenolics at more than trace levels.	**Phenolic**
Refers to a very aromatic wine with a high level of volatiles.	**Pungent**
Distinctive developed wood character of an old dessert wine stemming from a degree of oxidation. Highly desirable.	**Rancio**
Astringent, coarse tannin taste in red wines indicating lack of balance and maturity.	**Rough**
A well-balanced, smooth wine showing good fruit character.	**Round**
The most common manifestation of hydrogen sulphide in the form of mercaptan.	**Rubbery**
A touch of herbaceous or stalky character often found in young wines, particularly Pinot Noir, and usually a sign of potential quality.	**Sappy**
A wine having a highly aromatic smell, usually associated with flowers or fruits.	**Scented**
Agreeable and harmonious; opposite of astringent, harsh or rough.	**Smooth**
Wine with a pleasing finish, neither hard nor aggressive. May indicate fairly low acid levels, but not necessarily so.	**Soft**
Excessively acid, a character usually manifesting itself on the back of the palate.	**Sour**
Bitter character deriving from grape stalks, mainly appearing in red wines and indicative of poor winemaking.	**Stalky**
The framework of a wine contributed by the three basic building blocks of fruit, acid and tannin (and sometimes residual sugar), particularly relevant to red wines.	**Structure**
A wine with obvious, perhaps excessive, tannins; for a full explanation, see page 47.	**Tannic**
Akin to structure, but relevant to both white and red wines: may be smooth and satiny or more complex — like a tapestry — but should not be rough.	**Texture**
Lacking in body, almost watery and probably excessively acid.	**Thin**
1. A wine made from a single grape variety and bearing its name (noun).	**Varietal**
2. The flavour and aroma of a given grape variety (adjective).	

RIGHT: Greg Clayfield and a young Rouge Homme Cabernet Sauvignon.

Vinosity	A term relating to the strength of the grape character in a wine (though not necessarily the varietal character) and which typically develops with age. Denotes a desirable characteristic.
Volatility	Relating to the release of acetic acid and other esters, and which may be present to excess in a faulty wine.
TECHNICAL TERMS	Next come a few technical terms you are likely to frequently encounter.
Barrique	An oak barrel containing 225 litres (49 gallons) of wine, used almost exclusively in Burgundy and Bordeaux in France for maturation of wine, and increasingly used throughout Australia.
Baume	A scale for the measurement of grape sugar. One degree baume equals 1.8 per cent sugar, or 1.8 degrees brix (brix is a measurement of sugar).
Chaptalisation	The addition of sugar to partly fermented wine to increase the alcohol level, permitted in France but illegal in Australia.
Decant	The careful pouring of the contents of a bottle into a carafe or decanter to leave behind the crust or other deposits.
Fining	A method of clarifying young wines before bottling by the addition of beaten egg white, bentonite or other fining agent.

Wine that separates without pressing from grape skins after fermentation and which is generally more fruity and lower in tannin than the pressings that follow.	**Free-run**
An oak barrel containing 315 to 350 litres (68 to 76 gallons) of wine.	**Hogshead**
Muddy deposits which collect at the bottom of barrels and tanks primarily composed of dead yeast cells.	**Lees**
Technically, a fractional extraction of colouring and flavouring substances from the skins, pulp and pips of the grapes. It is achieved by leaving the juice in contact with these solid substances.	**Maceration**
In white-winemaking, unfermented grape juice; in red winemaking, the mixture of grape juice, skins and seeds before fermentation. During fermentation it is known as fermenting must.	**Must**
Literally, the power of hydrogen. In simple terms it is a logarithmic expression of the measurement of free hydrogen ions in solution. The lower the pH number, the higher the level of hydrogen ions and, in turn, the greater the available or useful acid. Table wine usually has a pH of between 3.1 and 3.6; white wines tend to have a slightly lower pH than reds. Low pH wines will usually age better than those with a higher pH.	**pH**
Wine recovered from pressing the skins, stalks and pips after fermentation. It is higher in tannin and may be deeper coloured. Often back-blended into free-run wine to add strength and colour.	**Pressings**
An oak barrel usually between 450 and 500 litres (98 to 109 gallons) in capacity.	**Puncheon**
Indentation at the base of a bottle originally introduced to strengthen it.	**Punt**
Unfermented grape sugar remaining in white wine in the form of glucose and fructose. Can be tasted at levels in excess of 5 grams per litre. Many so-called dry Rhine Rieslings have 6 to 7 grams per litre of residual sugar.	**Residual sugar**
A complex organic constituent of wine deriving chiefly from grape pips and stalks, and occurring in greater quantities in reds than in whites. Plays an important part in the self-clearing of young wines after fermentation, and thereafter in the period of maturation the wine requires: a full-bodied red, high in tannin, requires a longer period than does a lighter-bodied wine. Easily perceived in the taste of the wine by the slightly mouth-puckering, drying, furry sensation, particularly on the side of the tongue and on the gums. Some red winemakers add powdered tannin to wine to increase the tannin level artificially.	**Tannin**
The air space present in a bottle of wine between the cork and the surface of the wine. In old wines it is a fairly reliable indication of likely quality; the greater the ullage, the more suspect the wine.	**Ullage**
A container in which wine is fermented, made of stainless steel, concrete or oak.	**Vat**
The process of making wine.	**Vinification**

47

WINE FAULTS	Finally, we come to the principal wine faults.
Aldehyde/Aldehydic	A volatile fluid deriving from the oxidation of alcohol, present in most wines but undesirable in any appreciable quantity; hence, aldehydic. Acetaldehyde is a particular form of aldehyde.
Corked	A wine tainted by microscopic moulds growing in the pores of the cork. A corked wine will smell and taste sour, mouldy or possibly earthy.
Extractive	A coarse wine with excessive extract from skins and pips.
Madeirised	Oxidative change in white wines brought about by prolonged storage in warm conditions.
Mercaptan	Produced by ethyl mercaptan and ethyl sulphides in wine deriving from hydrogen sulphide and produced during the fermentation process. It manifests itself in a range of unpleasant odours ranging from burnt rubber to garlic, onion, gamy meat, stale cabbage and asparagus. While hydrogen sulphide can easily be removed, once mercaptan is formed, it is much more difficult to eliminate.
Oxidised	Refers to a wine that has been exposed to too much oxygen, resulting in loss of flavour and development of coarseness.
Volatile	A wine spoiled by an excess of acetic acid; it will have a sharp, pungent bouquet and a vinegary taste.

7 THE TASTE OF WINE

'I was convinced forty years ago — and the conviction remains to this day — that in wine tasting and in wine-talk there is an enormous amount of humbug.' T. G. SHAW, *WINE, THE VINE AND THE CELLAR* (1863)

Introduction

Michael Broadbent has written one of Mitchell Beazley's most successful pocket books on the subject, while the French master winemaker Professor Emile Peynaud has written a lengthy and fascinating book, *The Taste of Wine* (Macdonald & Co, 1987). Endeavouring to compress all of that material and more into one short chapter is not easy. After all, it is at the heart of the eternal fascination of wine, and at the heart of the eternal difficulty in describing its taste and communicating that description to others.

The three basic aspects of wine: colour, smell and taste

Whenever a full description is given of a wine, whether in a formal tasting note or in more general discussion, it will first describe the colour, then the smell (bouquet or aroma) and finally the taste. When a wine is judged in a show, each of these aspects is separately considered and allocated points: a maximum of three for colour, seven for bouquet and ten for palate (in other words, taste). It is the framework I shall use in the first part of this chapter.

COLOUR
Red wine colour

With red wine — much more than with white wine — you immediately become aware of the many facets of colour. Not only does it change markedly as the wine ages, but it may be bright or dull, light or dense. In other words, there is hue, intensity and clarity to consider. An expert looking at the colour of a red wine may well be able to guess its age, the grape variety and the region (or the climate) in which the grapes were grown. And the expert will certainly gain knowledge about the probable quality of the wine if he or she is told its age and variety — all this before the wine is smelt or tasted.

The changes of age

When it is young, a red wine made from Cabernet Sauvignon or Shiraz should be a deep, dark but clear (or bright) purple red. If it has the slightest blackish or bluish tinge, or if it is dull or both, it is highly probable its pH (see page 47) is too high, and the wine will not age well, quickly turning brown in colour and equally rapidly losing its fresh fruit taste. The good young wine will gradually lose its purple hue, turning dark red and ultimately brick red with a garnet rim or edge. If it is a Pinot Noir, the colour will at all times be much less dense and probably less purple; certainly it will lose its violet-purple tints more quickly and by mid-life will have a clear, light red-brown colour, fading to onion skin with great age.

White wine colour

ABOVE: Left to right – the colour of Pinot Noir, Shiraz and Cabernet Sauvignon, each of similar age (1-2 years).

BOUQUET

Notwithstanding the enormous advances made in analytical chemistry, the source of the yellow colour in white wine is still not fully understood, nor — in some instances — the reason for its progressive deepening with age. In this respect, white wines are the opposite of reds: whites become darker and deeper in colour as they age, reds become lighter. The colour change is from almost watery pale straw green through to yellow green (or lemon yellow) thence to golden yellow and finally gold. All of these changes are normal, and do not indicate anything is amiss. However, any brown or pink tinges are a sign of problems, usually oxidation or madeirisation. Any cloudiness (apart from sediment in very old wine) is likewise an indication something is amiss. Finally, oak-matured wines such as Chardonnay are likely to acquire more colour than a steel-fermented and early-bottled wine such as Riesling.

I have been a wine show judge for over fifteen years, and in that time have become thoroughly used to carefully assessing up to 200 wines a day (sometimes more) for three or four days on end. This has taught me several things. One is that wine judging is mentally very demanding, requiring total concentration, and that it is the brain which first becomes tired, rather than the nose or the tongue. Secondly, I have come to realise that 90 per cent of the total information I gain on 90 per cent of the wines in the judging comes from the bouquet. In other words, for nine out of ten wines, tasting the wine will basically do no more than

confirm what the bouquet has already told me, adding 10 per cent to my total knowledge and understanding (an important 10 per cent, it must be acknowledged). For the tenth wine, the palate will come as a major surprise, requiring a major revision, up or down, of the impression given by the bouquet.

The distinction between aroma and bouquet

A distinction is often made between aroma and bouquet: those who do make the distinction suggest that aroma is the smell of the grape (as manifested in the wine), while bouquet is that which develops as the wine ages and becomes more complex. Professor Peynaud prefers to make the distinction between primary aroma (the smell of the juice or must prior to fermentation), secondary aroma (the smell acquired during fermentation and which persists on a diminishing basis for some months or possibly years thereafter), and the tertiary aroma of a mature, bottle-aged wine which draws on the primary aroma, the secondary aroma and on the complex chemical changes which take place as the wine ages.

The aroma and flavour of wine

As I have suggested, the smells and the flavours of wine are very closely associated, and are bewildering in their complexity. By far the best shorthand graphic illustration of that range is the so-called wine aroma which was devised by Dr A. C. Noble for the American Society for Enology and Viticulture and which is reproduced (on page 52).

THE AROMA WHEEL

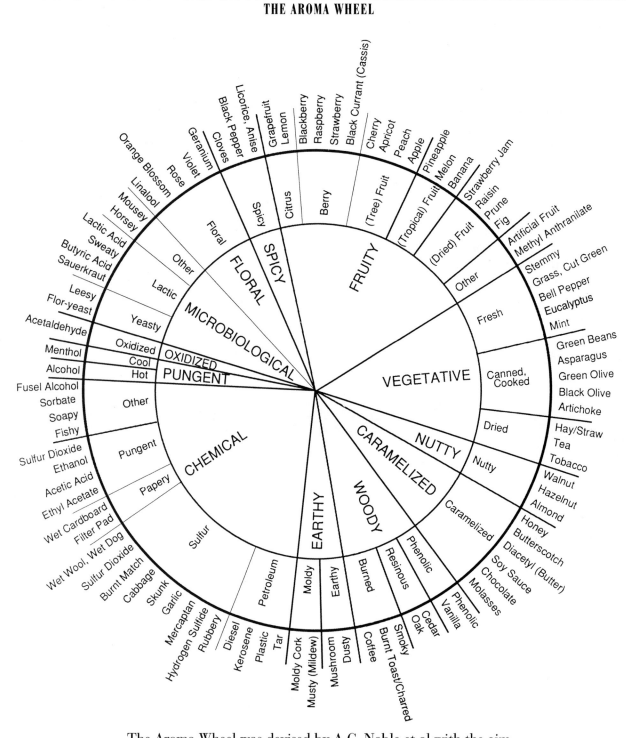

The Aroma Wheel was devised by A.C. Noble et al with the aim of limiting the use of vague or ambiguous wine tasting terms. Using the 'wheel', start from the inner circle — where the broad terms are listed — and work outwards to more specific taste descriptions. Copyright for the Aroma Wheel is held by the American Society for Enology and Viticulture.

For references see page 136

But aromas (and to a degree flavours) are underlain by the four primary tastes perceived by the tongue: sweetness, bitterness, saltiness and acidity. Anything we eat or drink may contain all or some of these primary tastes in varying combination and degree: the fascinating thing is that they are registered on different parts of the tongue, with the converse also holding true. In other words, large parts of the tongue are insensitive to one or more of the primary tastes.

One of the reasons we often talk about a sweet white wine 'finishing dry and crisp' is that sweetness is perceived only on the tip of the tongue. Similarly, the reason why bitter tastes in wine seem to come with the aftertaste ('a bitter finish' is a common expression) is that bitterness is perceived by the circumvallate papillae located so far back on the tongue that they only come into play as the wine is swallowed. Again, the reason why the experienced taster swills the wine around the mouth is that acidity is registered on the sides of and just underneath the tongue. Try for yourself the difference between simply holding the wine in the mouth (or swallowing it immediately) on the one hand, and swilling it around the mouth on the other.

TASTE
The basic constituents of taste

The way the tongue works

LEFT: *The first step in assessing the bouquet — agitating the glass.*

Tasting techniques

In similar fashion you may see (and hear) the expert noisily sucking in air through partially-opened lips while simultaneously holding wine in the mouth. This is because there are two routes of access to the olfactory mucosa and nerves, where 2 million neurones and 2000 fibre clusters relay messages to that part of the brain known as the olfactory bulb and which gives us our sense of smell. The two routes are directly through the nose, and via the retronasal route, the passage from the back of the throat going back up to the nasal cavity (and in which a grain of rice or a pea can so inconveniently lodge).

The steps in tasting: wine colour

And so the steps involved in tasting a wine fall into place. Assessing colour is largely a matter of common sense: ideally ensure a white background (the menu or a white card if you are in a restaurant will help) and either natural light or so-called daylight fluorescents (again, not practical in some circumstances — simply be aware of the distorting effect of low or coloured light). With a red wine, tilt the glass on an angle and observe the graduation of colour from the deepest part to the shallowest at the rim.

Assessing the bouquet

To smell the wine, it is highly desirable to agitate the contents of the glass. The expert effortlessly swirls the wine around and around; the novice attempting this for the first time is likely to empty half the glass on the surrounding table or bystanders. It is a knack which comes with practice, aided, however, by a glass such as the International Standards Organisation (ISO) tasting glass.

As you become more expert, you will realise there is a marked difference in the aroma detected if your nose is say a centimetre or two above the rim of the glass and that detected when the tip of the nose is within the glass. Not recommended is the inhaling of some of the liquid through the nose, a disaster which befalls even the expert from time to time.

RIGHT: Total concentration is required: the aroma tells you so much about the wine.

You should be endeavouring to identify three things: first, the fruit aromas present (usually identified by reference to other fruits, most of which you will find in the aroma wheel); secondly, the weight or intensity of the bouquet; and third, whether there are other smells or aromas present, be they pleasant (such as oak) or unpleasant (such as sulphur dioxide, hydrogen sulphide or aldehydes).

Now half fill the mouth with the wine, try to register the immediate impression, and then move the wine around inside your mouth — giving rise to another set of impressions. At this point you are left with a critical choice: to spit the wine out (hopefully into a receptacle provided for the purpose) or to swallow it. At most serious professional tastings, and certainly at all show judging, the wine will be spat out. Enough remains in the mouth to be automatically ingested with the reflex swallow which follows to register any bitterness.

What to look for

Assessing the palate

LEFT: The first taste.

RIGHT: It takes practice — lots of practice — but is an essential part of serious wine assessment.

The finish

Either way, you should concentrate on the mixed aroma and flavour perceived as you take your first breath after swallowing or spitting; it will almost certainly provide an additional perspective on the wine. Try, also, to estimate how long the flavour lingers: this is what is referred to as 'a long finish'.

The importance of balance

Overall, the impression should be of harmony and balance between the many complex flavours you will encounter. A good young wine may lack harmony, but it must have balance between the component parts: in other words, there may be rough edges and some of the flavours may seem to fall into compartments, but the size of those compartments must be appropriate to the future of the wine as it ages and softens. For example, it is idle to think an excessively tannic and astringent wine will be great in twenty years time. Certainly the tannins will soften, but so will the fruit: by the time the tannins are acceptable, the fruit needed to support them will have faded, and the wine will still be unbalanced. Predicting the future of a wine seems an impossible task to the novice; do not despair, that — and all the other tasting skills — will come to you in time. All you need is patience, perseverance and practice.

8 AUSTRALIAN WINE REGIONS

'In the year XXX. Good wine of the large irrigated terrain of the Temple of Rameses II in Per-Amon. The chief of the wine-dressers, Turmes.'
(EGYPTIAN WINE LABEL FROM A PYRAMID TOMB)

Introduction

Wine is grown in every State and Territory of Australia: the Northern Territory has Chateau Hornsby at Alice Springs, while the Australian Capital Territory has a string of wineries clustered around its perimeter run by the Canberra district vignerons. In this chapter I shall take you on a rapid-fire tour of each of the States and its wine-growing districts. If you wish to learn more, my *Wine Atlas of Australia and New Zealand* (Angus & Robertson, 1991) should provide the answers.

NEW SOUTH WALES

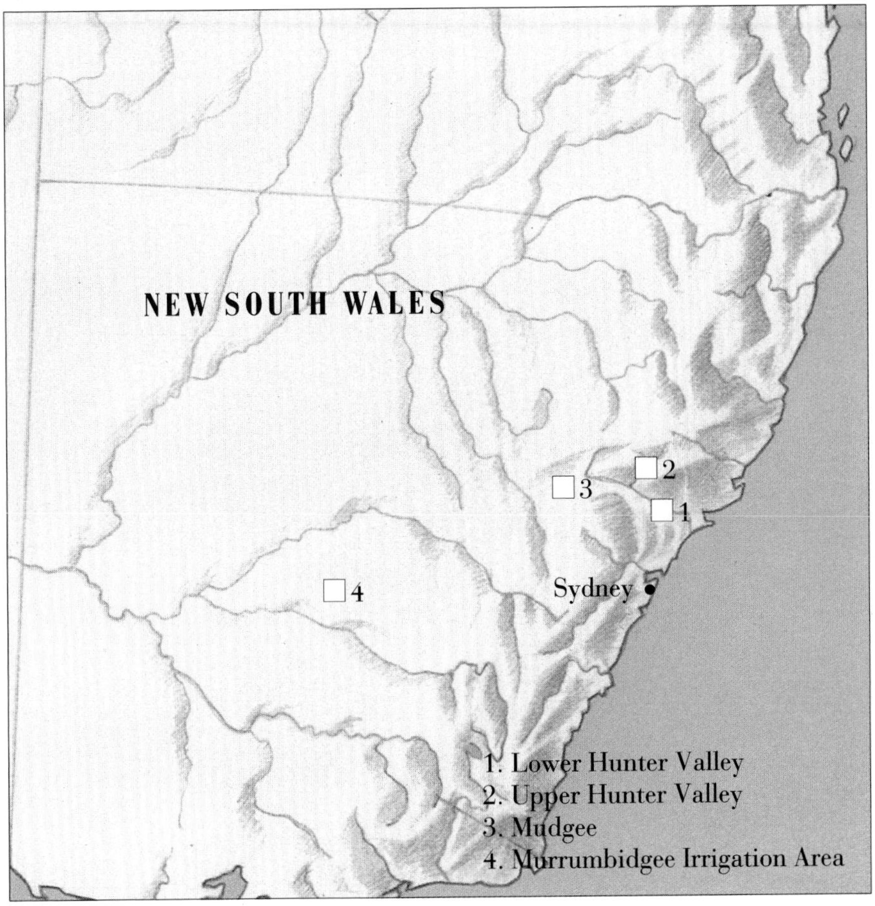

NEW SOUTH WALES
2
3
1
4
Sydney
1. Lower Hunter Valley
2. Upper Hunter Valley
3. Mudgee
4. Murrumbidgee Irrigation Area

New South Wales is the second most important wine-producing State, providing a little over 120 million litres (26 million gallons) of wine, or 27.5 per cent of the Australian total. The Murrumbidgee Irrigation Area was in turn responsible for two thirds of the State's total in 1990, the Hunter Valley contributing a mere 15 per cent. Almost as much wine as in the Hunter is produced along the Murray River between Swan Hill and Buronga in what is called the Sunraysia region, but it has only one small winery with its own label, Trentham Estate, and a substantial processing facility at Buronga owned by Thomas Hardy. The other significant wine-growing regions in descending order of importance are Mudgee, Canberra District, Hilltops (centred around Young) and Cowra. However, grapes are grown on either side of the Great Dividing Range all the way from Inverell in the north to Tumbarumba in the Snowy Mountains in the south.

HUNTER VALLEY

When we talk of the Hunter Valley, it is usually taken to mean the area north west of Cessnock which is home to almost fifty wineries, the most famous of which are Lindemans, McWilliams, Tyrrells, Rothbury, Tulloch and Wyndham Estate. This is in truth the Lower Hunter Valley; there is also the Upper Hunter Valley situated west of Muswellbrook, dominated by Rosemount Estate (and to a much lesser degree Mountarrow) and which is half the size of the Lower Hunter.

Traditionally, the Hunter Valley depended upon Semillon and Shiraz (or, as it is called there, Hermitage). In recent years Chardonnay has edged past Semillon, and Cabernet Sauvignon has

BELOW: The Brokenback Range rises above the dawn mist in a young Hunter Valley vineyard.

also become an important variety. The Upper Hunter is essentially a white wine region, producing one of Australia's most famous white wines, Rosemount Roxburgh Chardonnay. The Lower Hunter produces some of the greatest Semillon in the world, although, regrettably, much of the attention these days is focussed on Chardonnay. The wines of the Upper Hunter tend to mature fairly quickly; those of the Lower Hunter often repay extended cellaring — for ten, twenty or even more years. With age, all the wines have a certain softness: the whites are honeyed, the reds velvety, which I would like to think reflects the very warm climate of the valley.

MURRUMBIDGEE IRRIGATION AREA

The region is a major producer of white wine of modest quality which largely finds its way into wine casks. Semillon, Trebbiano and Muscat Gordo Blanco account for 50 per cent of the total plantings, and throughout the accent is on high yield, driven by extensive use of irrigation. The one premium wine, of world class, is De Bortoli Semillon Sauterne, made from heavily botrytis-infected grapes picked late in the season.

MUDGEE

Mudgee, an Aboriginal word meaning nest in the hills, has been quietly producing wine for over 130 years. Its total plantings of 668 hectares (1650 acres) compare with 939 hectares (2320 acres) for the Upper Hunter Valley, and leave no doubt that this is a significant area for premium wine production. The accent is on dark, rich and full-flavoured reds led by Cabernet Sauvignon, but the district makes some very good Chardonnay which is by far the most important white variety. Montrose, now part of the Orlando group, is much the largest winery, but a large percentage of the grapes grown in Mudgee make their way over the Great Dividing Range to the Lower and Upper Hunter, where Rosemount and Wyndham Estate are significant buyers.

VICTORIA

Judged by almost any standard, Victoria has been the most dynamic State during the past twenty five years. Since 1966 wine production has risen by almost 500 per cent from a little over 14 million litres to 70 million litres (3 million to 15 million gallons). Over the same period the number of licensed wineries has increased from twenty five to almost 200, spread across the length and breadth of the State. Space does not permit me to deal with each of the districts individually, so I shall group them into broad geographical areas.

NORTH-EAST VICTORIA AND THE MURRAY RIVER

North-east Victoria is the home of Australia's most unique wines: the fortified, lusciously sweet and intense muscats and tokays. The greatest of many fine producers are All Saints, Baileys, Chambers and Morris. The North-east is also home to Brown Brothers, which has more than kept in step with the overall growth in State production since 1960. By sourcing its grapes from a variety of regions, but increasingly from the hillsides of the King Valley, Brown Brothers has shown it is possible to produce high quality table wine in addition to the fortified wines for which the region is so justly famous. The other specialty of the region is the full-blooded reds, with Baileys leading the way.

ABOVE: The National Trust classified tower at Chateau Tahbilk, Victoria.

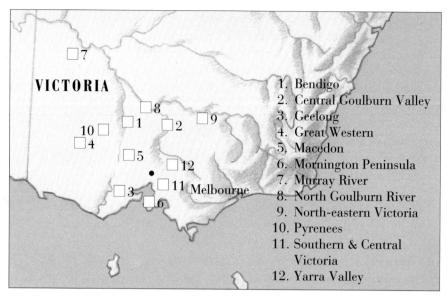

VICTORIA

1. Bendigo
2. Central Goulburn Valley
3. Geelong
4. Great Western
5. Macedon
6. Mornington Peninsula
7. Murray River
8. North Goulburn River
9. North-eastern Victoria
10. Pyrenees
11. Southern & Central Victoria
12. Yarra Valley

As you travel west along the Murray River, you come first to the northern end of the Goulburn Valley and to the headquarters of Tisdall at Echuca; a further 200 kilometres (124 miles) to the west and you arrive at Swan Hill, and ultimately another 200 kilometres as the crow flies, the Victorian Sunraysia region centred around Mildura. Here you will find Lindemans Karadoc Winery, the largest single winemaking facility in Australia, dwarfing the far older headquarters and principal winery of Mildara.

CENTRAL VICTORIA

Coming south to the centre of Victoria, and moving from east to west, you will find the Goulburn Valley (Mitchelton and Chateau Tahbilk), thence Bendigo (with seventeen wineries), then the Pyrenees (with seven wineries headed by Taltarni and Chateau Remy), and finally Great Western, where Seppelt has its Victorian base and chief sparkling winemaking facility — it is the largest winery in the region. This is emphatically red wine country, with Cabernet Sauvignon and Shiraz vying for supremacy: popular fashion no doubt favours Cabernet Sauvignon, but some of Australia's greatest Shiraz is grown and made here by wineries such as Mount Langi Ghiran, Bests, Mount Ida, Jasper Hill, Dalwhinnie, Chateau Tahbilk, Summerfield and Paul Osicka.

SOUTHERN VICTORIA

The Southern Victoria regions stretch from the western districts (centred on Portland and Drumborg) through to the Melbourne dress circle of the Yarra Valley, Mornington Peninsula, Geelong and South-west Gippsland, and ultimately across in the far east to East Gippsland. The climate has now graded from hot in the north, to warm in Central Victoria and to cool in Southern Victoria: cool not just by the standards of Australia, but by those of Europe. The wines are much finer and more elegant (some critics say delicate), with almost as much white wine produced as red. Chardonnay, Rhine Riesling and Sauvignon Blanc are the principal white wines, Cabernet Sauvignon, Merlot and Pinot Noir the principal reds. The Yarra Valley and Mornington Peninsula are two of the fastest-growing wine regions in Australia, with over sixty producers providing wines under their own labels. Twenty years ago there were none.

OPPOSITE: Autumn hues at Coldstream Hills in the late afternoon.

SOUTH AUSTRALIA

Throughout much of this century South Australia produced around 75 per cent of all Australian wine; however, since the end of the 1960s its share has slowly but steadily declined to the point where it now fluctuates at around 55 per cent. Obviously enough, despite the decline it is still by far the most important wine-producing State, and the South Australian Riverlands stretching along the Murray River from Renmark in the east to Waikerie in the west are truly the engine room of Australia. However, as in New South Wales, and to a lesser degree in Victoria, although the bulk of the wine comes from the irrigated Riverland vineyards, the most famous wines come from the four other principal districts: Barossa Valley, Coonawarra Padthaway, Southern Vales and the Clare Valley, all clustered in the south-east corner of the State.

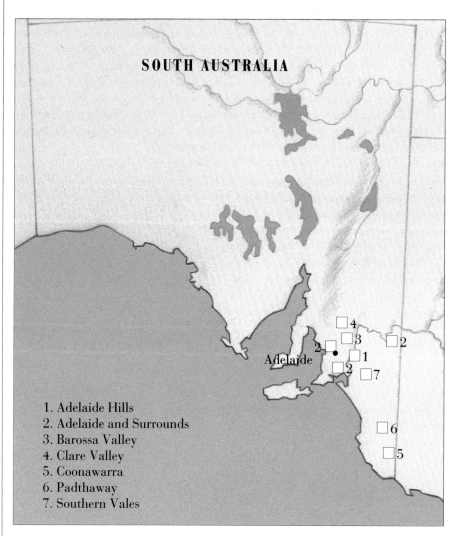

SOUTH AUSTRALIA

Adelaide

1. Adelaide Hills
2. Adelaide and Surrounds
3. Barossa Valley
4. Clare Valley
5. Coonawarra
6. Padthaway
7. Southern Vales

BAROSSA VALLEY

Without question this is the most famous of all Australian wine regions: it is a tourist delight with its strong German influence, stone buildings and picturesque scenery. It may be of limited importance viticulturally, with overall plantings on the decline, but it is home to almost all of Australia's largest wine companies, the most notable being Penfolds, Seppelt, Orlando, Leo Buring, Wolf Blass and Yalumba — and another thirty odd wineries of varying importance, including such well-known names as Krondorf, Peter Lehmann, Tollana, Saltram and Basedow.

Many of these wineries are supplied by grapes grown across the length and breadth of South Australia, so every style of wine is made in the Barossa Valley. The valley-grown wines are principally Rhine Riesling, Shiraz and Cabernet Sauvignon, all of which are generously flavoured.

CLARE VALLEY

The Clare Valley stands in the same sort of relationship to the Barossa Valley as Mudgee does to the Hunter Valley. It is much smaller than the Barossa Valley, is further from Adelaide, and its extreme beauty has been largely untouched by the twentieth century. It is only in relatively recent times that the major wine companies have acquired a significant presence there: Thomas Hardy now owns Leasingham, and Wolf Blass owns Quelltaler Estate (which it renamed Eaglehawk). The other twenty odd wineries are largely family run and owned, producing some of Australia's greatest Rhine Riesling, superb full-flavoured and long-lived Cabernet Sauvignon, and outstanding Shiraz.

SOUTHERN VALES

The Southern Vales have long since merged with the southwards push of Adelaide's suburbs: many famous vineyards of the 1950s are now covered with a sea of houses. As you travel south from Adelaide you first come to a group of half a dozen wineries at Reynella, the most famous and historic of which is beautiful Chateau Reynella, headquarters of the Thomas Hardy winemaking group. There is then a 15 kilometre (9 mile) break until you descend into its heartland, with more than thirty wineries clustered around McLaren Vale. This region has long been regarded as a specialist red wine area, producing massive (in terms of colour, alcohol and extract) red wines which were believed by nineteenth century doctors in England to have great medicinal and restorative powers. However, since the mid 1970s the region has shown a hitherto unsuspected capacity to produce excellent Chardonnay and Sauvignon Blanc.

LANGHORNE CREEK

On the other side of the Fleurieu Peninsula at another 30 or so kilometres (18 miles) to the south-east, is the Langhorne Creek region, with its own maritime-influenced cool climate and specialised growing conditions relying on winter flooding of the plains on which the vines sit. A surprising number of South Australia's larger wine companies have sourced substantial quantities of wine from this little-known and underrated sub-district.

COONAWARRA

In the far south-eastern corner of the State, and by a quirk falling just inside the South Australian rather than the Victorian border, are the twin districts of Coonawarra and Padthaway. Coonawarra is unchallenged as Australia's greatest red wine region, with twenty wine companies having vineyard holdings there, but far more buying grapes from the region and making the wine (typically) in the Barossa Valley, or even further afield. Despite the fact that the reputation of the district was forged between 1893 and 1950 on the basis of its Shiraz, it is for Cabernet Sauvignon that it is now best known. Needless to say, the quality of the Shiraz is also very high and it is also slowly gaining a reputation for Chardonnay. However, much of the Chardonnay and Pinot Noir grown in the region is used for sparkling

PETALUMA

1987 COONAWARRA

750ml

PRODUCE OF AUSTRALIA BOTTLED AT PICCADILLY SA

63

wine, and only Wynns, among the big producers, have had much success with the considerable quantities of Rhine Riesling which the district produces.

PADTHAWAY

If Coonawarra is justly famous for its reds, Padthaway is famous for its white wines, led by Chardonnay, but backed up by excellent Sauvignon Blanc and Rhine Riesling. All of the major Australian wine companies other than Orlando have vineyards in either or both of Padthaway and Coonawarra; Orlando is a major purchaser of grapes from both districts, leading literally hundreds of other purchases. In terms of overall production, Coonawarra and Padthaway combined are of the same size as the Barossa Valley; when quality is brought to account, the districts can claim to be South Australia's most important premium wine producers.

WESTERN AUSTRALIA

BELOW: Washing a barrel at Houghton Wines before refilling with wine.

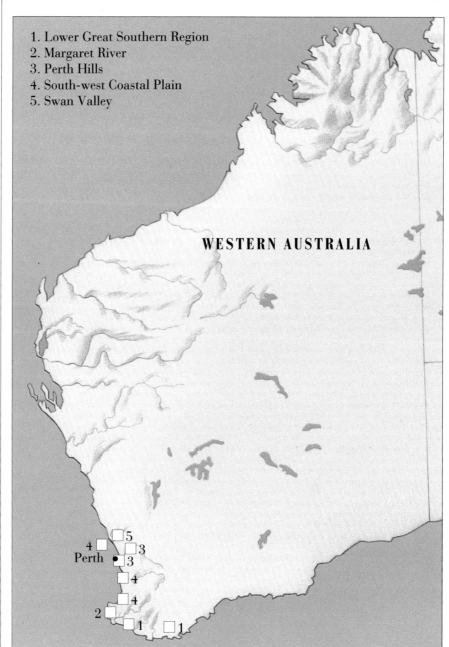

1. Lower Great Southern Region
2. Margaret River
3. Perth Hills
4. South-west Coastal Plain
5. Swan Valley

WESTERN AUSTRALIA

Perth

If one ignores some relatively small scale nineteenth century wine production, until 1966 viticulture in Western Australia was restricted to the Swan Valley. Since that time the Lower Great Southern region, the South-West Coastal Plain and the Margaret River have all been opened up, and now provide 67 per cent of the State total. There is as great a range of climate as one could imagine: the Swan Valley has the highest mean January temperature of any of the major wine-growing districts, the lowest summer rainfall and the most sunshine hours per day. At the other end of the spectrum is the strongly maritime-influenced climate of the vineyards in the far south-west corner of Australia around Denmark and Albany.

SWAN VALLEY

Houghton Wines sits aside the valley like a friendly colossus, producing Australia's number one selling dry white wine, Houghton White Burgundy. Despite the fact that Houghton was long owned by a British company rejoicing in the name of the Emu Wine Company before its acquisition by Thomas Hardy in 1976, viticulture in the valley has been the preserve of Yugoslavs, who came in two waves: the first around the turn of the century, the second after the Second World War. These days the Swan Valley is almost entirely given over to white wine production, with a significant part of its output (and that of the nearby Gin Gin Vineyards owned by Houghton) going to make Houghton White Burgundy.

MARGARET RIVER

BELOW: Vines and inter-planted cover crops weave a surreal pattern at Leeuwin Estate.

The Margaret River region captured the imagination of the Australian wine-buying public in the 1970s, and by some curious process, that fascination has now extended to visitors from overseas who have an interest in wine. The three areas such people pinpoint are the Hunter Valley, the Barossa Valley and the Margaret River, strange given the

relatively small production of the district and the absence of any major Australian wine company. The answer no doubt lies in the very particular beauty of the area, and the excellence of the wines produced by makers such as Cape Mentelle, Cullens, Leeuwin Estate, Moss Wood and Vasse Felix. After a surge of interest and development in the late 1960s and early 1970s, the pace slackened until the latter part of the 1980s, which has seen the number of wineries almost double. Whilst best known for its Cabernet Sauvignon, Margaret River can produce wonderful Shiraz, and has recently established a strong identity for its pungently grassy Semillon, which is often blended with Sauvignon Blanc and Chenin Blanc. Chardonnay, too, is rapidly growing in importance thanks to the recent arrivals on the scene and to the earlier success of Leeuwin Estate with this variety.

Lower Great Southern

This is a massive region which in the years to come will undoubtedly be split into three or four separate regions, each with its own acknowledged identity. It covers a vast surface area, forming a rectangle 150 kilometres (93 miles) deep and 100 kilometres (62 miles) wide, the four corners bounded by Albany in the south-east,

RIGHT: *Karrivale winery nestles at the foot of the granite hills of the Porongurups, north of Albany.*

Denmark in the south-west, Manjimup in the north-east and the Porongurups in the north-east. Not surprisingly, there is a great diversity in site, soil and climate: overall, fine, steely Rhine Riesling and austere, long-lived Cabernet Sauvignon are the outstanding wines of the region, but producers such as Plantagenet at Mount Barker and Wignalls at King River disturb the neat pattern by producing outstanding Chardonnay and (in the case of Wignalls particularly) some of the best Pinot Noir to be found outside of Victoria.

SOUTH WEST COASTAL PLAIN

This is another geographical oddity, stretching all the way from Bunbury in the south to Wanneroo in the north, united by the sandy soil upon which the vines are grown. Capel Vale and Leschenault in the south and Paul Conti in the north are the leading producers.

QUEENSLAND

Ignoring the curious outposts of viticulture at Roma and the Atherton Tablelands, grape growing in Queensland is concentrated in the Granite Belt district of the Darling Downs, following the New England Highway south of Stanthorpe to the New South Wales' border. The fourteen or so wineries are all small: only Ballandean Estate (with a production of around 5000 cases) enjoys national distribution. Overall, the district does best with pepper/spicy Shiraz and Semillon, although the dictates of current fashion draw attention to Chardonnay, Cabernet Sauvignon and Sauvignon Blanc. Grape growing is possible because of the elevation: the season starts very late, and finishes late, giving rise to claims by some that this is a cool climate region. In fact, high daytime temperatures make a nonsense of this claim, for the heat during the growing season is greater than that of Rutherglen in North-east Victoria.

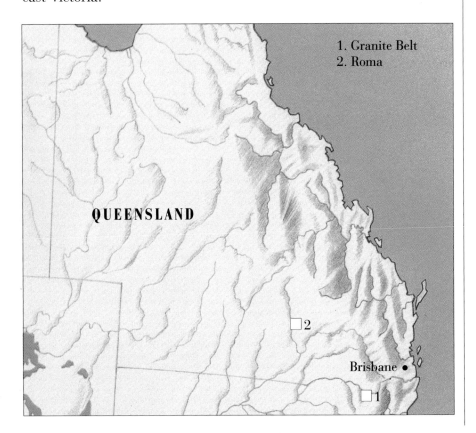

1. Granite Belt
2. Roma

QUEENSLAND

☐2

Brisbane ●

☐1

TASMANIA

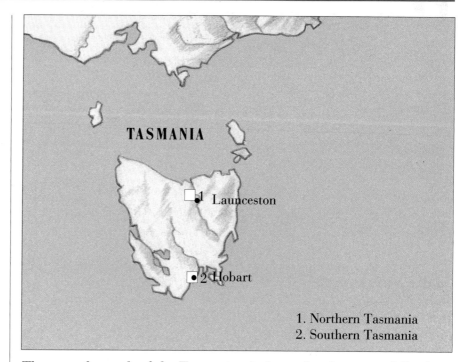

TASMANIA

1 Launceston

2 Hobart

1. Northern Tasmania
2. Southern Tasmania

ABOVE: Windswept skies above a Tasmanian vineyard.

The rate of growth of the Tasmanian industry has been painfully slow, notwithstanding the efforts of Moorilla Estate, Pipers Brook (brilliantly led by Dr Andrew Pirie) and Heemskerk, the three leading producers. There are four principal subdistricts: Pipers Brook and the Tamar Valley in the north, the East Coast (roughly half way up that coast), and the southern regions of the Derwent Valley and adjacent Coal River area. The surprising thing about Tasmania is the diversity of the climate, and the difficulty of making generalisations about which wines and which wine styles will do best. In broad terms, Chardonnay and Pinot Noir seem most suited to the Pipers Brook and Derwent Valley regions, Cabernet Sauvignon to the Tamar Valley, Rhine Riesling to most districts, while the East Coast and the Coal River areas (and perhaps the Tamar Valley) appear able to ripen almost all grapes to a satisfactory level. However, exceptions abound throughout, if only to prove the rule.

9 WINE SHOWS AND MEDALS

'The Jimmy Watson Trophy at the Royal Melbourne Show is worth $1 million in additional sales revenue to the winner of that trophy.' VARIOUS ANON.

Introduction

You need have only the slightest familiarity with or interest in wine to be aware of the importance of the Australian wine show system and the gold, silver and bronze medals which it bestows on wines. It is another thing again to properly understand the system, the way it works, and the true significance of medals.

The historical context

The wine show system goes back to the second half of the nineteenth century and to the foundation of the Agricultural Societies (now the Royal Agricultural Societies) in each capital city and in many towns. With the notable exception of gold, Australia's economy was firmly based on primary production, and the agricultural shows were of great importance. It was also the era of the great international exhibitions, and although these were based more on manufactured goods, wines (being long-life goods and transportable over long distances) were also a significant part of these exhibitions. From that time to the present, control of the Australian wine shows has rested with various district and capital city Agricultural Societies, rather than with the wine industry.

LEFT: Old show certificates: having the same fascination as old stamps.

A unique system

BELOW: *Yeringberg, Victoria, produced some of the most famous wines of the late nineteenth century.*

The purpose of the shows

Shortcomings of the system

Unbottled wines

Nowhere else in the world is there such a comprehensive (and all-important) system. In each State there are a series of regional shows, the more enlightened of which concentrate wholly or principally on the wines of that region, or at least of that State. In a perfect world these would act as formal steppingstones to the capital city show, with a medal award at the regional show a prerequisite to entry at the capital city show. The top of the pyramid would then become the Canberra National Wine Show. For a variety of complicated reasons, some valid, some not, this formal pyramid has not developed except for Canberra, which does require each wine to have won a medal at either a capital city or an approved regional show. But the basic structure is there nonetheless.

Much of the uninformed criticism of the show system stems from a lack of understanding of its historical context (in particular that it is controlled by the Agricultural Societies with their own agendas and aims) and more importantly, of the purpose of the wine show. In its conception and in its execution a wine show is organised for the benefit of the exhibitors, as a form of advanced education. It allows winemakers to have their wines assessed in complete anonymity by a panel of highly expert judges, and in the process of assessment, evaluated and rated against the comparable wines of their peers. It also gives the exhibitors the chance to taste both their wines and the medal-winning wines in each class after the results are published at the exhibitors' tasting which follows each show.

Seen in this light, the show system is not designed or intended for the benefit of consumers. But it is an expensive business to enter wine shows when all the costs are added up, and financial controllers of large companies like to obtain a return for their money. Enter the wine marketer, who sees the public relations opportunities in show success, keeps the financial controller happy, and flogs the system for all it is worth, making the consumer think it all happens for his or her benefit.

The shortcomings of the system principally affect the consumer: how does he or she know what relationship class 5 in the Royal Sydney Show bears to class 20 in the Royal Melbourne Show? What indeed does class 5 or class 20 mean? What were the other wines in the class? How many gold medals were awarded? In the real world, the consumer won't be able to find the answer to those questions, and the issue is whether it matters very much. For the reasons I give below, I don't think it does.

The real problem with the system has been the practice of awarding trophies and medals to wines which have not been bottled at the time of entry into the show. Canberra was the first show to ban the entry of unbottled wines; many of the other shows have now followed suit, or do not award medals, but simply give points. Yet the most famous red wine trophy of all — Melbourne's Jimmy Watson Trophy — is for a one-year-old red wine which, to date, has always been unbottled. The objection or difficulty is that the wine as finally bottled six or so months later may — for any number of reasons — be quite different to the wine entered in the show.

All wines are entered in shows with special labels and codes devised by the show organisers so that even if they were to see the bottles (which they do not) the judges would not know who made the wine. In fact the glasses are placed by stewards on numbered squares on each judge's table and it is this number (typically 1 to 100) which identifies the wine on the judge's scoring sheet. The only other identification is the class number: let us assume the class number is 5, and there are forty four wines in it, the full identification of each wine will be 5/1, 5/2 ... 5/43, 5/44. It is this number which will ultimately appear in the results catalogue, with the commercial name appearing alongside, and the points given and medal award, if any.

Each judge sits in a booth, and the class will be judged by the panel of three judges in complete silence. At the major shows there will be three panels of three judges each, presided over by the tenth judge, called the Chairman. Each panel is led by a senior judge, and when the panel has finished the class, each judge will call out his or her points for each wine. Not until all the points have been called and recorded will there be any discussion. In most instances, the points will be similar, and are simply averaged. If, however, there is a major discrepancy, or if a wine has been given gold medal points by one or two judges but not the other, the wine will be discussed and probably retasted. If the three judges are unable to come to agreement, the Chairman will be called in, and in almost all instances he or she will be the final arbiter. Right to the end, the judges will have no idea of the identity of the winemaker, ensuring complete impartiality.

How are wines judged?

BELOW: *The author tasting at a Sydney wine show.*

What is the significance of gold, silver and bronze medals?

Points are awarded to each wine out of a total of 20, with a maximum of 3 for colour and condition, 7 for bouquet and 10 for palate. Experienced judges go straight to their total points out of 20, associate judges (learning the ropes) allot marks in each section and arrive at the total that way. Half points can also be used. The following scale is used for medal awards:

> 15.5 – 16.5 inclusive: Bronze
> 17 –18 inclusive: Silver
> 18.5 – 20 inclusive: Gold

On average 3 per cent of all wines entered in a particular show will win a gold medal, 7 per cent a silver medal, and 23 per cent a bronze medal, for an overall success rate of around 33 per cent, seldom, if ever, rising above 40 per cent.

No absolute uniformity

The difference between a bronze and a silver medal is not great, nor is that between a silver and a gold. Those who expect to see exact uniformity between shows will be sadly disappointed: a typical track record for a very good wine will be one gold, two silver and four bronze medals; for a good wine a consistent swag of bronze medals interspersed with the occasional silver. Only the greatest wines will win gold medals in most of their show outings. If you see a wine with five or more gold medals you can be sure it is exceptional (provided it has won those medals after it is bottled).

The reasons for the variation will include interpretation of style, the overall quality of the other wines in the class, and the ultimate subjectivity of judging. So it is the overall record which counts, and it is for this reason I suggested earlier knowing exactly what each class number meant was relatively unimportant.

There are many other aspects to show judging — for example, do judges influence winemakers and wine styles, which are the best shows — which lie outside the scope of this book. For now, be confident in the overall integrity of the show system, and know that a wine which has won a sprinkling of medals is a good wine indeed.

10 DRY WHITE TABLE WINES

*'Montrachet should be drunk on the knees
with the head bared'.*

ALEXANDER DUMAS, WRITING OF THE GREATEST OF
THE WHITE WINES OF BURGUNDY

Introduction

Nowhere is the skill of Australian winemakers more evident than in their handling and making of dry white wine. Wine drinkers in this country take it for granted that white wine should be fresh, crisp, gently fruity and free from strange smells and tastes — in other words, clean. Cheap German, French or Italian white wine has none of these qualities: it is almost invariably stale, hard and smells and tastes more of old socks, boiled cabbage or cardboard than it does of grapes.

Variations in the level of aroma and taste

But this does not mean for one moment that all Australian dry white wines smell and taste much the same. The various grape varieties have very different levels and types of smell and taste, and the winemaker is able to build upon, subdue or reshape that smell and taste to a remarkable degree. The end result is, however, deliberate rather than accidental (as is the case with cheap European white wine).

As a general rule, the cheaper the Australian wine, the less the total volume of aroma and flavour: the exceptions are wines, often with a little sweetness, which have a proportion of Muscat Gordo Blanco or White Frontignac in their makeup. For a beginner, the absence of strong aroma and taste may be a good thing; on the other hand, the sweetness of a moselle-style often attracts the novice palate.

LEFT: The large, modern winery looks much like an oil refinery — but does the job.

73

DRY WHITE TABLE WINE

General Group Classification	Common Label Names	Grape Varieties Used	Specific Characteristics	General Comments
Aromatic light-bodied dry white wines	Riesling, Rhine Riesling, Traminer, Gewurztraminer, Dry Muscat, Frontignac	Rhine Riesling, Gewurztraminer, Muscat Gordo Blanco, White Frontignac	Floral, fresh and fruity, to be drunk young; only Rhine Riesling will repay cellaring.	Ideal for summer drinking and will appeal to those who do not like heavier oakier flavours; a little sweetness is a legitimate and often desirable part of the style. A full range of price and quality is to be expected.
Soft, fruity and flinty, light-to medium-bodied dry white wines	Chablis, White Burgundy, Fume Blanc, Semillon, Sauvignon Blanc, Chenin Blanc, Classic Dry White	Semillon, Sauvignon Blanc Chenin Blanc, Chardonnay, Colombard, Trebbiano (frequently blends of these grapes).	With the exception of Semillon and Sauvignon Blanc (and the occasional Fume Blanc), essentially bland, soft wines with no particular fruit flavour and usually only slight oak influence. Semillon improves greatly with bottle age.	Typically found in casks and at the cheapest end of the bottle wine range (especially Chablis and White Burgundy) and suited to those who prefer more neutral flavours. Semillon and Sauvignon Blanc wines are 'odd men out' in quality terms.
Medium- to full-bodied dry white wines	Chardonnay, Semillon (and the occasional high quality White Burgundy).	Chardonnay, Semillon, (Verdelho and Marsanne are rare examples).	Fleshy, full-bodied usually with pronounced oak influence; as the wine ages it becomes softer and more creamy, acquiring a buttery texture and toasty flavour. Semillon is the longest-lived.	Normally the most expensive dry white wines, although Chardonnay is increasingly found in low-priced bottles and will appear in casks. These low priced wines bear little resemblance in style or quality to the more expensive versions, the latter offering the weight and complexity to stand up to rich food.

AROMATIC LIGHT-BODIED WINES

The table (above) places dry white table wines into three main groups, the first being what is called in the wine show system, aromatic and light-bodied. All of the wines in this group will be made in much the same way: the whole aim of the winemaker is to preserve the natural aromas and flavours of the grape and present these in as pure a setting as possible.

How the wines are made

In practical terms this approach means scrupulous protection of the grape juice against oxidation before fermentation and equally scrupulous protection of the wine after fermentation. The cloudy grape juice which comes from the press will have been cold settled, filtered or centrifuged to absolute clarity before it is fermented; most makers will use a neutral yeast to start fermentation, which will be carried out very slowly at commensurately low temperatures in a stainless steel tank. The wine will be 'cleaned-up' (racked and filtered) as quickly as possible after fermentation is finished, and the wine bottled soon thereafter. At no stage will the wine have been placed in oak.

RHINE RIESLING

The best example of this style is Rhine Riesling, and the best Rhine Rieslings come from the Clare Valley, the Eden Valley (South Australia) and the Lower Great Southern region (Western Australia). While the wine — in common with the others in this group — is usually drunk while it is young, well-made examples repay cellaring for up to twenty years, the finest coming from Leo Buring.

When young, the aroma will typically show traces of passionfruit, lime and (if there has been some botrytis in the grapes) tropical fruit characters such as pineapple. As the wine ages, the citrus (lime) fruit will persist and build, and the smell of lightly-browned toast will often become quite pronounced. The taste and feel of the wine in the mouth will soften and fill out, the flavours basically tracking those of the bouquet. Since the latter part of the 1970s, most makers have chosen to leave a little unfermented sugar in the wine, typically 4 to 6 grammes per litre. This is at the threshhold of taste perception for even the most skilled taster, and is simply designed to lend support to the fruit flavour rather than simply add sweetness. It is also particularly useful in aiding the mouthfeel as the wine ages.

ABOVE: The morning dew helps all plants during the summer months.

GEWURZTRAMINER

Also often called Traminer, the variety produces the finest and most typical wine when grown in relatively cool climates. The maker always has a fine balancing act: if the grape becomes a little too ripe, or if the winemaking becomes a little too enthusiastic, the aroma and flavour can become overpowering with an oily, tannic finish to the taste which cloys to the point of unpleasantness. At the other extreme, the wine becomes altogether too delicate and watery, a pale image of itself.

The perfect Traminer (Orlando and Tolleys are two of the best South Australian producers) will have a highly floral bouquet with a strong, spicy scent which you can smell even as the wine is being poured. The flavour will also be spicy, sometimes with a strong taste of fresh lychee and a lesser citric background. With a few notable exceptions, the wine is best drunk when young.

MUSCAT AND FRONTIGNAC

Here there are no exceptions: these wines, with their piercing grapey aroma and flavour, simply have to be drunk when young. They are a brilliant coalescence of climate and technology, much admired in Europe but often under-appreciated here. You can literally taste the grape in the glass in wines such as Brown Brothers Dry Muscat Blanc, a gold medal winner at France's Expovin Show in 1991.

LIGHT TO MEDIUM-BODIED, SOFT, FRUITY AND FLINTY

This is a broad group of wines covering many varieties and styles: if you like, they are the middle-of-the-road wines, coming between the previous group (in which fruit aroma is all-important) and the third group of full-bodied wines (in which texture, weight and structure are all-important).

How the wines are made: skin contact

Because of the diversity of style, winemaking techniques vary somewhat. In Chapter 4 I gave a very broad outline of how white wine is made, and deliberately by-passed one stage known as skin contact. This technique is never used with the previous group of aromatic, light-bodied wines, sometimes used with this soft, medium-bodied group, and frequently used with the third group of full-bodied wines. It involves leaving the juice in contact with the skins after the grapes have been crushed and before they are pressed; the period of contact will vary between four and twenty four hours. The aim is to extract flavouring compounds (phenolics) from the grape skins; a secondary consequence is a marked deepening of the yellow colour of the wine, particularly once it is one or two years old.

I have often described the technique as a fly-now, pay-later approach. In the first twelve to eighteen months of the life of the wine it adds flavour, mouthfeel and texture, but thereafter the wine may become coarse, hard and oily. It may not, of course: much depends on the length of skin contact, and the amount of what I will loosely call natural flavour already present in the wine.

RIGHT: Old barrels in a traditional cellar; these days silicon bungs replace the wooden bungs and wax sealing shown here.

Oak treatment

The other chief difference between light-bodied wines and medium-bodied wines lies in the use of oak. It is probable that most of the wines you encounter in this group will have had some oak treatment. Once again, some explanation of this process is necessary. In Europe (for example in Germany for white wines and in France and Italy for red and some white wines) very old oak fermenters are used: these impart no oak flavour whatsoever to the wine. In parts of Italy, France and Portugal old oak barrels of varying size are subsequently used to mature the wine: once again, these do not contribute any oak flavour. The reason is two-fold: the oak flavour has long since been leached out (it lasts in the barrel on a diminishing basis for little more than five years), and secondly, deposits of tartrate build up which coat the inside of the barrel.

New oak

New oak (or oak less than five years old) will impart significant flavour. How much will depend on four things: the size of the barrel (the smaller the barrel, the more the flavour impact); the age and type of oak; whether the wine is fermented and matured in the barrel, or simply matured in it; and how long the wine is left in the barrel.

There is no suitable oak grown in Australia: all the oak is imported, chiefly from Europe (France, Germany, Yugoslavia and Portugal) and the United States. This makes oak treatment very expensive, and it does not matter greatly whether the barrel to be used is imported already fully assembled, or whether it is made in Australia from oak planks or simply re-assembled here.

By way of example, a good quality French barrique cost $800 in 1991, and held 265 bottles, giving a new oak cost of $3 a bottle, or $1.75 a bottle after allowing for the resale value of the used barrel.

This high cost has led both to the use of cheaper American oak, and more recently to the perfectly legal use of oak chips. These are tiny fragments of oak which are placed in the fermenter or in old cask (often held in a bag) and which liberate oak flavour. Another variation is a patented device called Innerstave, involving new oak planks being placed in the fermenter.

The lower the retail price of the wine, the less money the maker can afford to spend on oak. If skilfully used, oak chips or Innerstaves can do a remarkable job, and have been widely — if quietly — used in the industry for upwards of a decade. If you detect oak in a wine retailing for $6 or less, it is very probable this is the source of the oak.

These are two of the principal examples of what are called generic white wines as opposed to varietal white wines (where the name of the grape and the wine are one and the same). The names have been borrowed from France, and their use has declined in the face of criticism of the practice: the feeling is that we should develop our own names, and not steal those of France. While in that country they correspond to precisely defined areas and to a single grape (Chardonnay), here they have no legal or precise meaning.

If the wine is labelled chablis, it will probably have only very light oak flavour, if any; it will be made from a blend of fairly neutral grapes such as Trebbiano, early-picked irrigated Semillon and Colombard; and the tart, slightly green fruit flavour may be (incongruously) offset by a little sugar sweetness. It is a label which has always had strong acceptance in Sydney, due originally to the once great Lindemans Chablis and more recently to the Wyndham Estate Chablis Superior.

White burgundy will usually herald a rather fuller, riper and more oaky wine, typically made from Semillon. Basedows and Sevenhill make very good commercial examples, and are two of the few good wines to use the name.

Nor does fume blanc have any legal meaning: its saving grace is that the name was not stolen from the French, but borrowed from California where it was invented by Robert Mondavi to describe a wood-matured Sauvignon Blanc. While some believe that is the position here, the reality is often otherwise. The wine is occasionally made from Sauvignon Blanc, sometimes from a blend of Sauvignon

Sources of oak

The cost of oak

Oak chips

Quality and cost

CHABLIS AND WHITE BURGUNDY

CHABLIS

WHITE BURGUNDY

FUME BLANC

77

Blanc and other grapes, but will often contain no Sauvignon Blanc at all. It should show a smoky oak influence, and even if the wine is not made from Sauvignon Blanc, should show some of its grassy, herbal characteristics.

CLASSIC DRY WHITE

Classic dry white is a fairly recent arrival, used chiefly in the Margaret River to denote a blend of two or more of the following grapes: Chenin Blanc, Sauvignon Blanc, Semillon and Chardonnay. The blend gives a wine which often appears very similar to fume blancs from other regions, because all these varieties (other than Chardonnay) seem to have a slightly grassy/herbal taste when grown in the Margaret River.

SAUVIGNON BLANC

French chablis has always been regarded as the ultimate seafood wine (incidentally, I discuss the matching of wine and food in Chapter 19) but I cannot say the same of Australian chablis. If we make such a style, it is likely to be a crisp, non-oaked Sauvignon Blanc. However, the taste of the wine depends greatly on the region in which the grapes are grown, the way in which the canopy is managed, and the winemaking technique. It can be crisp, herbal, pungent and dry (in which case it is the seafood wine) or softer, more oaky and with sweeter, gooseberry/passionfruit flavour. The best have tremendous intensity, and are wines of real quality.

SEMILLON

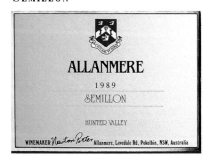

ALLANMERE

1989

SEMILLON

HUNTER VALLEY

WINEMAKER *Newton Potter* Allanmere, Lovedale Rd, Pokolbin, NSW, Australia

With Semillon we come to the only wine in this group which really repays cellaring, particularly if it has been made without the use of oak in the manner of the classic Hunter wines from Lindemans, Rothbury, McWilliams and Tyrrells. When they are young, these wines give but the barest glimpse of their potential; they are typically low in alcohol (around 10 per cent or 2–3 per cent less than Chardonnay) and have a slightly thin, grassy taste and little or no aroma. With ten or more years bottle age a miraculous transformation occurs: the wine gains complexity, weight and flavour, turning a brilliant green gold, acquiring the aroma of honey on toast and a buttery-nutty flavour. For all the world the wine seems to have been matured in new oak, when, traditionally, it will have had no oak at all.

MEDIUM- TO FULL-BODIED WHITE WINES

Semillon demonstrates just how difficult it really is to categorise wines and put them into pigeonholes. For a particular Semillon may well start life as a light to medium-bodied wine (and win wine show medals as such) but finish its life winning wine show trophies as a full-bodied dry white: countless Lindemans Hunter River Semillons from the 1960s and from 1970 made just that transition.

CHARDONNAY

But it is true this group of white wines increasingly centres around Chardonnay, and despite the prophecies of the Jeremiahs, will continue to do so in the future. Just because Lindemans can make a single 3 million litre (65 000 gallons) blend of Bin 65 Chardonnay (which is 4 million bottles) selling for $5 a bottle, or Woodleys can produce Queen Adelaide Chardonnay — made without oak but with a little residual sugar — at the same price, does not mean the days of premium quality, high-priced Chardonnay are at an end. Equally, just because there are those who are rediscovering the delights of good

LEFT: *Stages in the development of Chardonnay: left, the fermenting wine; middle, after five weeks in barrel; right, the finished wine.*

ABOVE: *A still life composed by nature.*

Rhine Riesling, Semillon or whatever after an overdose of Chardonnay, does not mean they have foresworn drinking Chardonnay again. Believe it, Chardonnay is here to stay, and stay at the top.

But we will see much greater diversification in the style of Chardonnay as well as in its price. Chardonnay is the most wonderfully flexible grape, bowing gracefully to the influences of climate, soil, viticultural practice and winemaking techniques, but always maintaining a recognisable identity.

The different styles of Chardonnay

Earlier in this chapter I have explained skin contact and the use and effect of oak. If you take a Chardonnay carefully grown in a warm region — the Hunter Valley, McLaren Vale or parts of the Riverlands — subject it to extended skin contact, barrel-ferment it in a mixture of new French and American oak barriques, and give it extended lees contact (see pages 37–8), the resulting wine will be variously described as a blockbuster, as a Dolly Parton special, as peaches-and-cream or whatever.

The big, rich style

Bottled before the end of the year of its vintage, and released early the following year, it will already be buttercup yellow, and will quickly deepen to golden yellow. It will have a honeyed, peachy aroma, masses of peachy flavour and a creamy, buttery texture. If it is a particularly good example, it will have cleansing acidity on the finish, and will not cloy. In this year following vintage it will win gold medals with ease, and (very likely) receive rave reviews in London, New York and Stockholm. But while it blooms lusciously, for most connoisseurs its flower will quickly fade: the colour becomes too deep, and the flavours become rather coarse and oily.

Superb but short-lived

If on the other hand you take a Chardonnay grown in a cool area such as Padthaway, South Australia, give it a brief (two to three hour) period of skin contact, barrel-ferment it in new French oak (say

Elegant, long-lived styles

79

Vosges) and make sure it is not over-oaked (by removal from oak or back-blending a portion fermented and kept in stainless steel), you will have a wine which will develop slowly and graciously, often taking between three and five years to reach its optimum. The downside is that the wine will be overshadowed by the much bigger and more obvious style described above when it is a one to two-year-old — and this precisely when it will be sold and consumed. (Over 90 per cent of all wine is consumed within 24 hours of purchase.)

The in-between style

In the end result, the more intelligent makers chose an in-between style, balancing the richness of the fruit against the winemaking technique. In other words, if they are taking grapes from a warm area, they will reduce the time of skin contact, possibly pick some of the grapes a little earlier than normal and perhaps reduce the time in barrel. Those taking grapes from a cool area may take precisely the opposite approach.

The perfect style

A perfect full-bodied white wine is the white equivalent of a light- to medium-bodied dry red. It will have complexity of aroma and taste which goes beyond the simple flavour of the grapes used; it will have structure and texture encompassing both fruit and tannins; it will age gracefully in bottle; and it will have the depth to carry almost any food. In the view of most connoisseurs (the Germans and Swiss excepted) it is the greatest dry white wine.

11 SWEET WHITE TABLE WINES

'The Germans are exceedingly fond of Rhine wines; they are put up in tall, slender bottles, and are considered a pleasant beverage. One tells them from vinegar by the label.' MARK TWAIN

It is highly probable that the first wine you tasted, and even more certain that the first wine you enjoyed tasting, was a slightly sweet white wine in the style of Leibfrauwine or Ben Ean Moselle. If your taste has graduated to dry whites and dry reds, it is probable you will be slightly embarrassed as you recollect your entry to the world of wine. I believe it lies behind the subsequent rejection of sweet wine by so many regular wine drinkers, who associate all sweet wines with the bland, gently sugary style they first tasted.

The sugar and acid balance of these wines conforms closely to that of popular carbonated soft drinks such as Sunkist Orange, Solo and so forth. One obvious advantage of the wines is the alcohol they contain, although winemakers would no doubt argue there are other bonuses too. But the similarity points to the purpose and function of these wines: they are soft, refreshing and undemanding.

The sweetness comes from unfermented grape sugar: the winemaker stops the wine from fermenting to dryness by chilling and filtering it, simultaneously adjusting the sulphur dioxide level to keep

LIGHT-BODIED, SEMI-SWEET WINES

MOSELLE AND SPATLESE STYLES

LEFT: Petaluma and the Piccadilly Valley — the ideal cool climate area for botrytised Rhine Riesling.

SWEET WHITE TABLE WINE

General Group Classification	Common Label Names	Grape Varieties Used	Specific Characteristics	General Comments
Light-bodied aromatic semi-sweet wines	Moselle, Late Harvest, Spatlese, brands such as Ben Ean, Liebfrauwein	Riesling, White Frontignac, Gewurztraminer, Muscat of Alexandria, Muscat Gordo Blanco, Chenin Blanc	Distinctly fruity aroma when at their best, bland and watery at their least. The sweetness is not marked, and should merge with the flavour. Should have a crisp finish.	A once very popular segment, now largely restricted to casks and low-priced bottles. For all that, remains the ideal entry point for many first-time wine drinkers.
Light-bodied aromatic sweet wines	Auslese, Autumn Harvest	Riesling, Gewurztraminer, Orange Muscat Flora, Chenin Blanc	Fruity aroma, strong fruit flavour with marked sweetness balanced by acidity.	Again, a segment declining in importance; the wines are fuller and sweeter, and are largely restricted to bottles.
Medium-bodied aromatic wines, very sweet	Botrytis(ed), Beerenauslese, Trockenbeerenauslese, brands such as Noble Riesling	Riesling (occasionally others)	Intense piercing aroma, lime, tropical fruits, apricot; intense flavour and fruit, with tingling lingering acidity.	Made from botrytis-infected grapes harvested late in the season, typically grown in cool areas. Almost invariably high quality, but with a limited market.
Full-bodied sweet wines	Sauternes, Porphyry (botrytis(ed))	Semillon, Sauvignon Blanc	Complex fruit and oak aroma and taste, very rich and sweet with many flavours; balancing acidity.	Historically made from non-botrytised Semillon (Porphry or Sauternes) but the best examples now made from heavily botrytised Semillon grown in the Murrumbidgee Irrigation Area.

the wine fresh and helping prevent any risk of ongoing yeast or bacterial activity. If the wines are made from varieties such as Frontignac or Muscat Gordo Blanco (perhaps labelled Lexia or Frontignac) they will have an intense grape aroma and flavour: Australia makes some of the best examples in the world of this type of wine, even if they do not receive much recognition in this country. If, however, they are made from other varieties, there will be a low level of fruit flavour. There are two reasons for this. First, the makers recognise that positive flavour is not wanted by the majority of consumers of this type of wine; second, the wines are cheap, and made from very high-yielding Riverland vines which simply do not provide intense flavour, the taste basically deriving from the residual sugar.

LIGHT-BODIED, AROMATIC SWEET WINES

One moves up a notch with these wines: there will be a concurrent increase in both the level of fruit (or grape) flavour and of residual sugar. I discuss the meaning and effect of botrytis later in this chapter: suffice it to say that traditionally these wines were made without the influence of botrytis. The grapes are usually harvested well after those destined to make dry white wine, and hence have higher sugar levels. Rhine Riesling is by far the most commonly used variety, and over the past twenty five years Leo Buring has produced a magnificent array of Reserve Bin wines under the hand of its recently-retired master winemaker John Vickery. These wines reach the peak of their power after ten years in bottle, and can live for up to twenty years. Most, it is true, are consumed when much younger, and likewise only a few rival the quality of the old Leo Buring wines.

Here it becomes necessary to explain botrytis and how it works. It is a mould (variously called by its scientific name *botrytis cinerea*, *edelfaule* in Germany and *pouriturre noble* in France) which attacks the skin of the grape. The organism makes tiny holes in the skin, allowing moisture — in the form of water — to escape, thereby concentrating the sugar, acid and flavouring constituents which remain the flesh. Initially, botrytis simply causes a brown-grey discolouration of the skin; by the time it is fully developed it covers the entire bunch in a very unappetising furry green-grey mould. It needs very specific temperature and humidity conditions to work perfectly: if it is too dry, too cold or too hot it will cease to be active; if it is too wet or too humid, it will run riot along with other mould and rot activity, thereby entirely destroying the bunch.

Wines which have been made from botrytised grapes have a distinctive, often penetrating aroma, and an unusual intensity of flavour. Just how penetrating and how intense will depend on the degree to which the botrytis has done its work. The greater the level of infection, the higher the aroma and flavour and the sweeter the wine. At extreme levels it may be difficult to tell what variety of grape was used: a strong apricot aroma and apricot-peach-cumquat flavour will intervene — which is not the least unpleasant, I hasten to add. Acidity, too, increases, both balancing and intensifying the flavour.

Most of these wines will have been made from botrytised Rhine Riesling, typically grown in a cool area such as Padthaway, Coonawarra or the Adelaide Hills. Particular brands may appear intermittently, such as Hardy's Padthaway Beerenauslese Riesling under the Collection Label, Petaluma Botrytis (from Coonawarra), Seppelt Auslese, Heggies and Pewsey Vale Botrytis Riesling. The reason for the irregular appearance is simply the unreliable nature of botrytis: this in turn adds substantially to the already-high cost of producing the wine, made high in the years in which the mould is successfully active because of the much reduced yield of juice per tonne of grapes (half or less of the normal yield).

An alternative and less risky method, which is also very useful in areas where the climate is too dry, too cool or too hot for botrytis to work, is called cordon or cane cutting. The vine's canes which are carrying the bunches are cut at their base, but left on the vine, held in place by the trellis. This causes the cane (or branch) to transfer moisture from the grapes back into the wood and the leaves, and gradually results in the grapes partially shrivelling and raisining. The resultant wine is less complex than one made from botrytised grapes, but has a high level of flavour.

A final method, used extensively in New Zealand but less commonly in Australia, is to partially freeze the grape juice before the onset of fermentation: pure water freezes first, and the frozen ice is separated from the juice. This technique, called freeze concentration, can be used with botrytis-affected juice, in which case the wine may be every bit as complex as a 'naturally' concentrated wine.

The role of botrytis

ABOVE: European wasps attracted by the extra sugar in the brown, botrytised grapes.

The effect of botrytis

MEDIUM-BODIED VERY SWEET AROMATIC WINES

Cordon-cut wines

Freeze concentration

FULL-BODIED SWEET WHITES

These wines are most commonly made from Semillon, the first point of difference from the preceding group. The second difference is that they will receive oak maturation, and very probably be barrel fermented in new oak. These days all of the best wines (with de Bortoli having a reputation second to none) are made from botrytised Semillon, much of it coming from the Murrumbidgee Irrigation Area.

PORPHYRY AND OLD-STYLE SAUTERNES

The traditional method — exemplified by the old Lindemans Hunter River Porphyrys and the McWilliams Sauternes from the same district — was to take a fairly common and undistinguished dry base wine and add mistelle to it, mistelle being a concentrated but unfermented (and hence very sweet) grape juice. The wine was then allowed to mature in bottle for many years: in 1991, for example, the 1956 Lindemans Reserve Porphyry and the 1962 Penfolds Bin 414 Sauternes were still both superb, albeit with a totally unique (to Australia) mixture of camphor, vanilla and honey.

Such wines are a dying breed in the face of the fairly abundant supplies of botrytised Semillon from the Murrumbidgee Irrigation Area and the infinitely greater complexity, bite and verve such wines have.

The taste of great sweet wines

It is to that bite and verve I turn in conclusion. Whether the wine is an unwooded botrytised Rhine Riesling of Beerenauslese sweetness or an oaked, luscious botrytised Semillon it will have certain things in common.

First and foremost, it will have an extraordinarily intense aroma and taste. Next, the mouthfilling sweetness of the wine will flood the senses as you first taste the wine. Then as you swallow it, tingling acidity will take over to give the wine balance and — amazingly — leave the mouth fresh and clean, almost as if the wine was not sweet at all.

These wines are normally sold in half bottles simply because a little goes such a long way. As I say, they are expensive to produce, and the purchase cost is necessarily higher than that of dry white wine. In reality, they rank among the great wine bargains in Australia today; you owe it to yourself to buy and taste a half bottle or two, and share the experience with your friends. It is a subject to which I return in Chapter 19.

De Bortoli Wines

SAUTERNES
Australian Botrytis Semillon

375 ml   PRODUCT OF AUSTRALIA   13.0% ALC/VOL

12 DRY RED TABLE WINES

'One never tires of summer sunsets; they are always beautiful and yet they are never quite the same. That is also the secret of the appeal which Claret has for all wine lovers; it is the most perfectly balanced wine and ever in a new garb; harmony without monotony.'

ANDRÉ SIMON

Introduction

It was not until 1975 that white wine sales overtook those of red wine, the subsequent eclipse being mirrored both in other parts of the New World (such as the United States) and to a lesser degree in the Old World producers such as France. In Australia red wine sales have grown only slightly since 1975, yet since 1980 the share of bottled red wine sales has doubled, and the share of red wine casks declined markedly. Thus bottles account for 50 per cent of red wine sales, but less than 25 per cent of white wine sales (where casks are dominant).

This differential is simply a reflection of the fact that for the serious wine drinker, good red wine is the ultimate pleasure. On the other side of the coin, medium to full-bodied red wines come as something of a challenge to the novice wine drinker, who may well be put off by the strength and (apparent) astringency of such wines.

ROSÉ

For this reason, rosé (and some light-bodied red wines) are a good starting point. In truth, a rosé has more in common with white wine than it has with red, notwithstanding its colour and notwithstanding that it is made from red grapes. After the grapes have been crushed, the juice is allowed to remain in contact with the skins for long enough to extract the light but vivid purple colour which is such an attractive part of Australian rosé style, but not long enough to pick up the tannins and the weight of a conventional red wine (which come from the anthocyanins concentrated in the skin of the grape).

The wine is then pressed off the skins, and fermented at cool temperatures in stainless steel in the same fashion as an aromatic white wine such as Riesling. Oak plays no part in the making of a rosé, which is cleaned up and bottled as soon as practicable after it has finished fermenting, and placed on the market by around August in the year of its vintage.

The market is dominated by Houghton Rosé, made in the Swan Valley of Western Australia from early-picked Cabernet Sauvignon. This wine wins all of the gold medals and trophies at the national shows, and is quite simply superb year in, year out. Smaller makers of note include Mount Hurtle and Charles Melton Rosé of Virginia, which both make Rosé from the traditional grape Grenache, and Miramar and Taltarni.

DRY RED TABLE WINE

General Group Classification	Common Label Names	Grape Varieties Used	Specific Characteristics	General Comments
Rosé	Rosé, Saigneé	Cabernet Sauvignon, Grenache, Pinot Noir	Scented, fresh, fruity aroma; palate may be dry or slightly sweet, but must be crisp and fresh.	The cross-over between red and white wines, which is ideally suited to summer drinking and should be much more popular than it is.
Light-bodied dry red	Pinot Noir, Cab Mac, Beaujolais (previously), Nouveau, Light Red	Pinot Noir, Gamay Grenache, Shiraz Malbec, Cabernet Sauvignon	Pronounced fragrant fruity bouquet; light but intense fruit-driven flavour; low tannin levels. Oak usually plays a minor support role. Strawberry and plum are dominant fruit flavours.	A sector of growing interest and importance, due in part to Pinot Noir and in part to perseverance with Beaujolais-type winemaking techniques. Ideal lunch or summer wines.
Medium-bodied dry red Soft finish	Burgundy, Hermitage, Shiraz, Cabernet Shiraz, Cabernet Sauvignon plus brand names e.g. Jacob's Creek, Wolf Blass Yellow Label, Jamiesons Run etc.	Shiraz, Cabernet Sauvignon, Malbec, Merlot or blends of the above	Fruit and oak both play an important role; there should be a certain softness in the wine from the bouquet all the way through to the finish, which in particular should be soft, though with ample tannins. Cherry, dark cherry and raspberry are main fruit flavours with spicy characters in Shiraz.	The most important part of the red wine market in Australia, typifying Australian red wine style. Varietal blends and brand names are dominant, particularly at the cheaper end of the market and in casks. Soft, easy drinking reds for all occasions.
Full-bodied dry red Firm finish	Claret, Shiraz, Cabernet Sauvignon, plus brand names	Cabernet Sauvignon, Shiraz	Powerful, often quite astringent aroma in young wines, matched by mouth-puckering, drying tannins on the finish. The essential balance is provided by strong dark berry fruit — black-current, cassis, mulberry, sour cherry.	The serious end of the wine-market, normally found only in bottles, and then in the middle/ upper price levels. Long-lived wines which have to be given time to mature to show their best, shining in winter dinner parties.

At the other end of the scale, with distinct sweetness, is Seppelt's Spritzig Rosé and the various cask rosés, headed as ever by Orlando Coolabah Rosé.

SAIGNÉE

A few makers are providing a rosé made by fermenting juice which is bled (the French word is *saignée*) or run off, that is removed, from the vat of crushed red grapes and juice. The vat is allowed to ferment in the usual way, the object of the juice run-off being to concentrate the colour and flavour of the remaining wine. This technique has been used by some Coonawarra makers for a number of years (notably Wynns) and more recently by makers of Pinot Noir (such as Bannockburn and Coldstream Hills) and even Merlot (Dromana Estate) who ferment the run-off juice separately and then market it as a varietal Pinot Noir Rosé or Saignée or Merlot Rosé.

LIGHT-BODIED DRY REDS

With these wines we move unequivocally into red wine territory, but not so far as to alienate the new wine drinker or the person who finds conventional red wines do not agree with him or her. Either because of the genetic make-up of the variety (in the case of Pinot Noir) or the method of making (notably in the instance of carbonic maceration) the tannin levels of these wines are very much lower and the fruity freshness very much more obvious than in conventional red wine.

The use of carbonic maceration as a winemaking technique takes us back to what must have been the dawn of wine, when primitive humans stored grapes in clay pots as a winter food source and found that the juice which oozed from the grapes during the storage had a strange taste and a wonderful effect on his or her feeling of well being. Two things had happened: first, the grapes had fed on themselves by converting sugar to the carbon dioxide they needed to stay alive, in the process also creating alcohol. This is a purely internal reaction triggered by enzymes naturally present in the grapes, and lies at the heart of the carbonic maceration process. Second, as the skin of the grapes weakened and juice ran out, wild yeasts present on the grapes' skin interacted with the juice. This, combined with the crushing of the lower levels of the stored grapes by the grapes above them, led to a simultaneous conventional alcoholic fermentation.

It is a curious sidelight that full scientific understanding of the internal (enzymatic) fermentation did not come until well after the Second World War (in the course of research into long-term cold storage of table grapes) and that a particularly sophisticated use of the technique was developed and patented in Australia by the Hickinbotham family. They developed one of our most popular beaujolais styles under the Cab Mac brand, now owned by Mitchelton.

The use of the word beaujolais is no longer permitted on Australian wine in the wake of a long legal battle by the French producers to protect their reputation and sole right to the name. So we see imaginative names such as Cab Mac, April Red, Summer Red and more straightforward versions such as Nouveau, Light Dry Red, Soft Red and so forth. All of these wines have a soft but fresh fruity flavour (often with a spicy/gamy edge) and are best drunk when they are young. They should be slightly chilled on a hot summer's day. By one means or another (and there are a large number of permutations and combinations available) it is probable whole bunches of grapes will have been partially fermented before crushing and/or pressing, depending on the technique, and that the wine will have been pressed well before it finishes fermentation. If, as seems the case, Australians will not take rosé to their hearts, surely these light red wines must become increasingly popular, as they are so suited to our warm climate.

Pinot Noir is a somewhat specialised varietal form of light dry red. While many of the carbonic maceration variants are used in its making, a large part of the character of the wine derives from the genetic make-up of the grape: it has much lower anthocyanin levels than other grapes, and those present are subtly different in any event. The result is a wine which is much lighter in colour and lower in tannin than other red wines, characteristics which have led to considerable confusion and misunderstandings by expert and novice alike.

If Pinot Noir is grown in a warm climate, if it is allowed to become super-ripe, and if, say, 20 per cent of Shiraz pressings is added to it (perfectly legal, as I explain in Chapter 14), Pinot Noir can be made to

Carbonic maceration

BEAUJOLAIS STYLES

PINOT NOIR

What Pinot Noir should not taste like

ABOVE: Netting is expensive but the only fully effective protection against attack by birds.

The cool climate dress circle

look and taste like any other warm-grown medium-bodied dry red wine. The expert may guess it is a blend of Shiraz and something else, but may be hard-pressed to say whether it is Cabernet Sauvignon, Malbec, Grenache or Pinot Noir. The result may be a perfectly pleasant and acceptable dry red, but it is most emphatically *not* what true Pinot Noir is or should be about.

The best Pinot Noirs are grown in some of the coolest regions of Australia: the dress-circle around Melbourne (the Yarra Valley, Mornington Peninsula, Geelong and South Gippsland), in Tasmania, the Adelaide Hills and at Albany in the Lower Great Southern Region of Western Australia. As with the red wine of Burgundy, France (also made from Pinot Noir) the wine is light red in colour, and assumes a brick or onion skin edge within a relatively few years. The aroma of strawberries, plums, rhubarb and violets is intense, sometimes showing a touch of spicy new oak and a sappy green cut or edge from tannins drawn from the stalks left in the fermenter. The wine is never thick, heavy or tannic on the palate, but the flavour should be piercing and long-lasting after the wine is swallowed. The fruit flavours are in the strawberry to plum range, sometimes with cherry manifesting itself. The majority of Australian Pinot Noirs are at their best within two to five years of vintage, though exceptional examples live longer.

This was the principal red wine style made in Australia for most of this century, with Shiraz the base building block. In retrospect, these wines often lacked individuality and finesse: they had ample flavour but had an overriding roasted character and lacked freshness, perhaps due to insufficient acid. The introduction of the use of new small oak barrels, a better understanding of the role of pH and acid, and the progressive opening up of the cooler growing regions have all played a part in transforming the style and quality of these wines.

If there is a single example of the traditional style (albeit with a modern face) it is Penfolds Kalimna Bin 28. In the middle come wines such as Wolf Blass Yellow Label and Mildara Jamiesons Run, with Orlando Jacobs Creek at the lighter end of the spectrum. These brands alone account for a significant percentage of Australian sales of bottled red wine, and are also significant contributors to exports.

While, as I suggest, there are significant differences in the weight and depth of flavour of these wines, there are even more features in common. For a start, American oak is an important contributor to flavour (and texture), with French oak rarely contributing much. The reason for the use of American oak is partly economic (it is much cheaper than French) and partly stylistic (the sweet vanillan flavour is ideally suited to the wine). Next, in all except a few wines such as Bin 28 the tannins will be kept at a relatively low level, as will the acidity. The resultant softness — most evident in all the Wolf Blass wines — means that the wine will be ready to drink when it is first sold. This softness and roundness is aided by the blend of grapes used in most of these wines: Shiraz, Cabernet Sauvignon and Malbec being the most common, Merlot less so.

This provides another face to the medium-bodied dry red: when the wines are very young, the finish may be anything but soft, but bottle-age transforms them. Lindemans, McWilliams, Tyrrell and Tulloch have always been household names in Sydney, which has in turn long been the major Australian wine market. In turn, the dry reds of these companies have fairly and squarely rested upon Shiraz, the vagaries of labelling and marketing resulting in the use of the names burgundy (notably by Lindemans) and hermitage (by the other makers). Here oak plays a much less important role, the wine acquiring its distinctive gently earthy, softly leathery aroma and flavour as it ages — characters described as being like a sweaty saddle after a hard day's ride, abbreviated to sweaty saddle. In more exaggerated cases the wine can acquire a leathery/gravelly/tarry smell and taste: this used to be accepted as regional character, but is now generally recognised as deriving from mercaptan, and as faulty winemaking.

Many of Coonawarra's red wines, whether made from Shiraz or Cabernet Sauvignon or a blend of these or other grapes, also fall into this group — or a closely allied group described as 'medium-bodied firm finish' in wine show schedules. While they start off life bearing no resemblance whatsoever to Hunter Valley reds, after twenty or more years the likeness can become quite remarkable. That, at least, has

MEDIUM-BODIED DRY REDS

The major brands

The formula used to make them

HUNTER VALLEY SHIRAZ

COONAWARRA

been the track record of the Coonawarra and Hunter wines of the 1950s and 1960s; it remains to be seen whether the rather different Coonawarra reds of the 1980s will develop in the same way. (That difference is due to the greater use of new oak in Coonawarra, and to the new-generation viticultural practices.)

FULL-BODIED DRY RED FIRM FINISH

The distinction between full-bodied firm finish dry reds and the previous group is not necessarily as clearcut as the terminology might suggest. Nor is there much comfort to be drawn from looking at the grape varieties: Shiraz-based wines can be found in either group, as can Cabernet Sauvignon.

PENFOLDS GRANGE HERMITAGE

The most outstanding example of full-bodied Shiraz is Australia's greatest red wine, Penfolds Grange Hermitage. It is not a wine for beginners or for the faint hearted, and at $60 a bottle for the current (1986) release in late 1991, is beyond the budget of many experienced wine drinkers. Nonetheless, anyone seriously interested in wine should try to at least taste Grange Hermitage — the most obvious way being to share the bottle (and its cost) with a group of friends.

Not for the faint-hearted

ABOVE: Max Schubert.

But do not be disappointed if you do not enjoy the experience. It can be compared to a weekend driver of a four cylinder family car being placed behind the wheel of a Formula One racing car, if not quite as dangerous. The colour of a five-year-old and hence young Grange is dense, the bouquet packed with dark berry fruit and strong vanillan/charred oak, the palate almost impossibly crammed with flavour, finishing with powerful, astringent tannins and a whisker of volatile acidity. It is, if you like, a caricature of a red wine, larger than life in all respects. The sheer genius of its creator, Max Schubert, and the skills of those who have followed in his footsteps, only becomes obvious once the wine passes its tenth birthday, growing for up to another decade thereafter. Beyond that time the rate of change slows as the wine enters the plateau of maturity, exemplified by the sheer perfection of the 1955 Grange drunk in 1991.

OTHER FULL-BODIED SHIRAZ

It is altogether curious how little attempt there has been to duplicate the style of Grange: in the past few years Jim Barry Wines has launched The Armagh, a Clare Valley Shiraz given opulent oak-treatment (and sophisticated packaging and labelling) which is far from a poor effort. The very old, low-yielding, non-irrigated Barossa Valley vines which provide the core of Grange have also given such famous wines as Henschke Hill of Grace, St Hallett Old Block Shiraz and the less well known Rockford Basket Press Shiraz, monumental wines in their own right but of different style.

THE VICTORIAN COLLECTION

Yet another dimension comes from the biggest wines of Central Victoria. Those of Chateau Tahbilk are massive in body, tannin and extract, having much more affinity with the legendary blood-and-thunder reds of North-east Victoria exemplified by Baileys. Curiously, Chateau Tahbilk's rare 1860 Shiraz, made entirely from vines planted in that year, is somewhat more elegant and less tannic than the standard Shiraz of the winery.

LEFT: *Some very old Shiraz vines can still bear a good crop.*

Cooler climate

As one moves west across Central Victoria from the Goulburn Valley to Bendigo, more great Shiraz is encountered, here often having a distinctive taste of mint and eucalypt, lower tannin levels but no less weight — Walkershire, Jasper Hill, Balgownie, Mount Ida and Passing Clouds are among the best. As you progress further to Great Western, the pepper/spice of even cooler regions starts to manifest itself, sometimes in the best wines of Seppelt and invariably in those of Mount Langi Ghiran — the last viewed by many as the best producer of cool climate Shiraz in Australia. As you twist southwards to Macedon, the pepper/spice characters become more obvious again, but the fruit weight, vinosity and richness of Mount Langi Ghiran is not there. This pepper/spice character is found in most of the great Rhône Valley hermitage-based wines; both there and in Australia it diminishes with age, but is a highly desirable part of the character of the young wine.

CABERNET SAUVIGNON

But it is Cabernet Sauvignon which produces most of the wines in this group, simply because of the innate firmness and astringency of the variety which reflects itself most obviously and persistently on the finish of the wine.

The effect of vintage variation — the French experience

However, a word of caution here. So far I have avoided any discussion of the effect of different climatic conditions from one year to the next, commonly called vintage variation. Before the advent of modern sprays developed to combat the growth of rot and mould in nearly-ripe grapes, the variation in French vintages used to be dramatic. The Cabernet-based wines produced in Bordeaux in 1963, 1965 and 1968 were virtually undrinkable: some makers refused to sell them under

BELOW: A bottle of this wine, made around 1915, was sheer perfection when drunk in early 1992.

their own name, others reduced the quantity selected for release to a tiny percentage of normal, and all of the wines were sold for a fraction of the price of wines from the good vintages of 1962 and 1966. Changes in weather patterns and better sprays have narrowed the quality gap somewhat, but no one would compare the Bordeaux wines of 1984 and 1987 with those of 1985, 1986 and 1989: the former are light to medium-bodied, the latter full-bodied.

The Australian experience

In the same way, the Cabernet Sauvignons of Coonawarra from 1987 and 1989 are distinctly lighter in body than those of 1986, 1988, 1990 and 1991; likewise, the Hunter Valley had to wait for five years after 1986 for a year in which truly rich red wines could be produced as was the case in 1991. So be aware that any neat pigeonholing is liable to be upset from time to time by the vagaries of nature, and the effect of vintage variation.

The best Cabernet Sauvignons

In any discussion of Australian Cabernet Sauvignon four names are sure to crop up: Penfolds Bin 707 (a blend of Barossa Valley and Coonawarra), Wynns John Riddoch (Coonawarra), Lindemans St George (Coonawarra) and Petaluma (Coonawarra) — attesting at once to the importance of Coonawarra and the dominance of the South Australian Brewing Group, which owns the first three brands. Here French oak takes over from American, perfectly matching and complementing the mixture of blackcurrant sweetness and green leaf astringency of great Cabernet.

Cabernet Sauvignon: the great traveller

But Cabernet Sauvignon is one of the great travellers, and can produce majestic full-bodied wines in almost every combination of soil and climate. Thus there is the Margaret River (with Cape Mentelle, Moss Wood and Cullen to the fore); the Lower Great Southern (Alkoomi, Goundrey and Plantagenet), the Southern Vales (Coriole, Normans and Seaview), the Barossa Valley (Elderton, Peter Lehmann, Saltram and Seppelt's Dorrien) the Clare Valley (Mitchell, Sevenhill, Skillogalee, Tim Knappstein and Wendouree, the last making some of the most concentrated and long-lived of all Australian reds); the Yarra Valley (Mount Mary, Oakridge, Seville Estate, Yarra Yering and Yeringberg); Central Victoria (Balgowie, Bests, Chateau Tahbilk, Dalwhinnie, Mount Langi Ghiran, Redbank and Taltarni); the Hunter Valley (Brokenwood Graveyard, Lake's Folly, great though seldom more than medium-bodied, and Wyndham Estate); and finally Mudgee (Huntington Estate and Montrose).

All of these wines share above-average weight and flavour without becoming heavy or clumsy. All will repay cellaring for at least a decade, many for twice as long. They are wines for a winter's night, an up-market barbeque (if young) or the great dinner party (if fully mature). They are the red wines to which most people turn once they have tried all the others.

13 SPARKLING AND FORTIFIED WINES

'I drink it when I'm happy and when I'm sad. Sometimes I drink it when I'm alone. When I have company I consider it obligatory. I trifle with it if I'm not hungry and drink it when I am. Otherwise I never touch it — unless I'm thirsty.'

MADAME LILY BOLLINGER ON CHAMPAGNE

Right at the outset, I shall declare my hand: I do not believe any sparkling wine made in Australia or in any part of the world outside Champagne, France should be called champagne. This is so despite the fact that since 1963 the written laws of Australia have specifically permitted the use of the word (in certain circumstances which I discuss hereunder), and that Australian winemakers have in fact used the term champagne for a century or more. It is even more ironical that as the quality of the best Australian sparkling wines (using the Methode Champenoise) has improved out of all sight, and grows ever closer to true champagne, the use or misuse of that name is increasingly limited to the cheaper, lower quality sparkling wines.

Under Australian law, a producer can call wine champagne if the wine is fermented in a bottle, and spends at least six months on its yeast lees, a term I explain in a moment. There is no requirement that any particular grape varieties be used, and no requirement that the wine be fermented in the bottle in which it is sold — the true Methode Champenoise. The distinction between this method and the so-called transfer method appears from the table (page 95), but there are those who would argue that the distinction is at the least irrelevant, and that indeed the transfer method leads to a greater consistency of quality.

Whether that is so or not, the fact remains that all French champagne and nearly all the finest Australian sparkling wines are made using the Methode Champenoise (often called MC for short). The emergence of these wines in Australia has been very much a development of the 1980s, hastened in the second half of the decade by the involvement of some of the famous French champagne makers, or houses, such as Bollinger (with Petaluma), Roederer (with Heemskerk in Tasmania), and Moet et Chandon (its own multi-million development in the Yarra Valley). Remy Martin, the owners of Krug, have had a far longer involvement with Chateau Remy, but the genesis of that was brandy, not sparkling wine.

Introduction

The technical meaning of the word champagne in Australia

METHODE CHAMPENOISE: THE FRENCH CONNECTION

RIGHT: The traditional — underground cellars at Taltarni.

The importance of cool climate Chardonnay and Pinot Noir

Yeast lees autolysis

ABOVE: The modern — gyropalettes for shaking down yeast lees at Olive Farm.

There is good cause to suggest that the real turning point came before the arrival of the French, thanks principally to Seppelt and to a lesser degree Seaview. These companies recognised that not only was the use of Chardonnay and Pinot Noir essential if high quality sparkling wine was to be made, but that those grapes had to be grown in cool regions. Only that way could wine be made which had the delicate yet intense flavour which would slowly and subtly take shape and flower as the two or three years maturation on yeast lees passed by.

I promised I would explain what is the significance of yeast lees, and now do so, throwing in the word autolysis for good measure. The yeast which is added (along with the sugar) to create the secondary fermentation — which is in turn responsible for the *mousse* (bubbles or effervescence) in the finished wine — falls to the bottom of the bottle and dies as the fermentation finishes. The dead yeast cells form a small creamy/muddy deposit, and after six to nine months they break down, liberating nitrogen compounds and amino acids into the wine. This process is called autolysis, and is accepted as giving much of the bready complexity and the slightly creamy texture shared by all great sparkling wines. And it has to be admitted by even the greatest Francophile that the effect will be uninfluenced by the subsequent disgorgement of each bottle and individual removal of the sediment

SPARKLING WINES

Name of Making	Mechanics of Making	Grapes Used	Common Label	General Comments
Methode Champenoise	The dry base wine is fermented in the usual fashion, and then blended, usually with different grape varieties from different regions. The blended wine is bottled, and the sugar and yeast added to initiate the secondary fermentation. After a minimum of six months maturation the sediment (yeast lees) is removed through disgorgement and the liqueur d'expedition added. The key to Methode Champenoise is fermentation in *this* bottle, rather than *the* bottle.	Chardonnay, Pinot Noir, Pinot Meuniere	Methode Champenoise, MC, Brut, brand names such as Salinger, Croser or producer names such as Domaine Chandon. The word Champagne may be used but is usually only found on the cheaper versions, and then in conjunction with a brand name.	The very best sparkling wines are made in this way, almost always bearing a vintage and are usually two or three years old when sold.
Transfer Method	The primary fermentation, blending and secondary fermentation are done in exactly the same way as for Methode Champenoise. After maturation the total contents (including sediment) of each bottle are decanted into pressurised tanks, filtered, liqueured and returned to new bottles.	Chardonnay, Pinot Noir, Pinot Meuniere, Semillon, Chenin Blanc, Colombard, Trebbiano	Similar to above, often identical — including the term Methode Champenoise, and frequently Champagne. Major brands such as Fleur de Lys, Carrington, Minchinbury.	Used for a wide range of quality (and style) from premium through to high volume, low-priced brands such as Minchinbury.
Charmat or Tank Fermentation	The dry base wine is placed in a pressure tank; sugar and yeast are added, causing the second fermentation. The wine is then chilled and filtered, transferred to a second pressure tank; the liqueur d'expedition is then added, and the wine filtered once again before bottling.	Muscat Gordo Blanco, Trebbiano, Chenin Blanc, Colombard, Semillon	Various brand names such as Bodega, Summerwine, Jean Pierre, etc; most Spumantes are made this way. The word Champagne may not be used.	These are the most commonly encountered very cheap sparkling wines, selling for $2.99 or even less in 1991. Many are quite sweet, especially the Spumantes.
Carbonated	The base wine is sweetened by the addition of liqueur d'expedition (or sugar), chilled to 0°C, and then injected with a stream of carbon dioxide in a baffled vertical cylinder, with the wine moving in one direction, the carbon dioxide in the other.	Sultana, Palomino, Muscat Gordo Blanco, Trebbiano, the cheapest available.	Almost entirely brand names such as Croupier; also Spumante; also many flavoured wines (Sparkling Peach and so forth).	The once-famous Bests Baby Cham was made this way; now of importance for the cheapest end of the market and for flavoured wines.

under the Methode Champenoise, or in bulk under the transfer method. But that is a story, and an argument, for another day.

The finest examples of this style are Croser, Domaine Chandon, Seaview, Edmond Mazure, Seppelt Salinger and Seppelt Vintage Brut. They are distinctly Australian, being cleaner, fruitier and somehow fresher than champagne; alas, they are also less complex, shorter-lived and less challenging than champagne.

TRANSFER METHOD

This method is used to make the vast bulk of adequate to very good Australian sparkling wine. Its success — and that of sparkling wine producers generally — is best gauged by the phenomenal growth in bottled-fermented sparkling wine sales over the past decade, rising from less than 5 million litres (1.09 million gallons) (550 000 cases) a year in 1980/81 to over 25 million litres (5.5 million gallons) (2 770 000 cases) in 1990/91. The total market for sparkling wine of all kinds (bottle fermented, bulk fermented, carbonated and flavoured) is 35.6 million litres (7.7 million gallons), and hence bottle-fermented sales account for 72 per cent of that total.

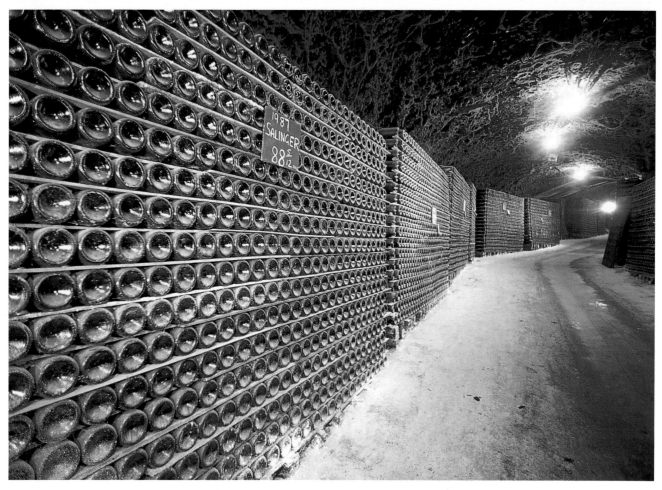

Why have sales increased so much?

ABOVE: The famous underground drives at Seppelt are both functional and beautiful.

Style and quality

Enough dry statistics. Why has the sparkling wine market out-performed all other wine sales in the decade? Market demand, of course, but what has created that demand? Intense competition between the major producers has been a major cause: at the start of the decade Seaview, Penfolds and Seppelt were separately owned and correctly saw the growth potential. They built even larger and more efficient sparkling wine plants; they progressively lifted the quality of their products moving from bulk fermentation to bottle-fermented sparkling wine; notwithstanding the much greater cost of producing bottle-fermented sparkling wine, they kept prices largely unchanged (and hence dramatically decreased in real terms) over that decade; and despite the low profit margins have developed very attractive (and expensive) labelling and packaging.

But the quality of the wines relative to price is also exceptional: by the start of the 1990s this had been accepted in major overseas markets, and in particular the United Kingdom which now imports, for example, 75 per cent of the total production of Seppelt Salinger. Basically, you get what you pay for. The higher-priced wines have great length of flavour and intensity, elegance combined with power, and finish crisp and dry. The lower-priced wines are made from lesser grape varieties in two distinct styles: the dry wines with neutral flavours, the sweeter wines with the grapey, spicy flavours of the muscat family.

Here the price comes down further, and connoisseurs and expert judges would say so does the quality. Apart from the fact that the best grape varieties (Chardonnay and Pinot Noir) are never used, the key difference lies in the fact that the wine spends no time on yeast lees, and is sold within weeks of having been made. So the creamy complexity of bottle fermented sparkling wine is altogether absent. This is not likely to worry those who buy and drink these wines, even if bulk-fermented wines are a fast-disappearing category now accounting for less than 10 per cent of total sparkling wine sales.

Most are spumante style, quite sweet and with a strong grapey taste. Their great advantage is the broadness of their appeal: even those who rarely drink wine of any kind are likely to enjoy, or at least tolerate, the taste. Hence their appeal at weddings and similar functions.

These are the cheapest of all the sparkling wines, and are invariably sweet. Some spumantes are made this way, but it is the fruit (peach, passionfruit and so forth) flavoured versions which are most popular, and have indeed seen quite remarkable growth in the market share of carbonated wines: the sales in 1990/91 were 3.3 million litres (72 000 gallons), up 85 per cent over the preceding year and nearly matching those of bulk-fermented wines. They clearly act as a bridge between soft drinks and wine in its traditional sense; and although purists may sneer at such creations, like wine coolers, they have strong appeal to a section of the market which is too important to be ignored.

Rosé does not fit into any one particular making method or price segment: pink champagne (as it is commonly called) comes in all shapes, sizes and prices. However, in all cases it will be made by adding a small percentage of strongly-coloured red wine to the base white wine, with the subseqent treatment being exactly the same for the corresponding white sparkling wine. At the premium end, there may well be more Pinot Noir used in the base wine; at the bottom end, the finished wine will probably be even sweeter than its white counterpart. But at the risk of generalising, the main difference is optical: that ever-so-appealing pink colour.

Sparkling burgundies are an altogether different story. They are bottle-fermented wines using a conventional red wine base. The most famous example, Seppelt Great Western Sparkling Burgundy, has always used Shiraz, and most other makers follow this pattern. One or two use Cabernet Sauvignon, but Shiraz seems to work best. As the museum wines of Seppelt have proved, sparkling burgundy can be extremely long-lived: the 1944 and 1946 vintages were still superb at the start of the 1990s, the only problem being their extreme scarcity. Still, one can always dream.

Some of the greatest, and the most individual, Australian wines fall in this group. What is more, until the 1960s, more than 70 per cent of all wine made in Australia was fortified; it was the backbone of the industry (and of exports) throughout the first half of the century. Most was relatively young sweet sherry and tawny port of mediocre quality; exports in particular did nothing for the reputation of Australia.

BULK FERMENTED

CARBONATED AND FLAVOURED WINE

ROSÉ AND SPARKLING BURGUNDY

FORTIFIED WINES

FORTIFIED WINES

Type of Wine	Method of Making	Grapes Used	Direct Makers	General Comments
Dry or Flor Sherry	Differs from other types of fortified wine, because the base wine is made like a table wine and fermented to dryness before being lightly fortified (to 15%) and placed in cask, where it is innoculated with flor yeast. After 12–18 months contact with the flor, it is removed, blended, refortified to 18% and given further cask maturation before bottling at around 7 years.	Palomino, Pedro Ximinez	Seppelt, Lindemans, McWilliams, Mildara, Yalumba	Flor Fino Sherry, often called just Fino Sherry, is a sadly neglected and under-rated aperitif style wine. Served chilled in summer it is a delicious drink; the quality is extremely high, second only to Spain.
Amontillado Sherry	Made in the same way, but left in cask for much longer before bottling, gaining a softer, nuttier flavour and texture. Spends 10–20 years in barrel. Like flor, there will be a complex blending system (called a solera) involving the partial emptying of barrels of increasing age, with younger wine replacing that drawn off.	As above	As above	Perhaps the easiest of all sherries to drink and enjoy; there is a hint of honeyed, nutty sweetness on the mid-palate followed by a cleansing, drying finish. It is a year-round drink of considerable style.
Oloroso and Amoroso Sherry	Not influenced by flor, and fortified to 18% at the outset. Spends 10–30 years in the barrel, and will be sweetened by the addition of highly concentrated grape juice. Solera system is essential.	As above	Seppelt, Lindemans, McWilliams	Little known wines which are quite superb; the sweetness and richness of the mid-palate are offset by the cleansing cut of the finish. A winter aperitif or equally good at the end of the meal.
Cream Sherry	A commercial style which is fortified to 18% and spends only a relatively short time in barrel, often without a solera system, relying instead on straight-forward sweet fruit flavour.	Muscat Gordo Blanco	McWilliams, Lindemans, Penfolds	An unashamedly commercial style, sometimes called cream and some-times simply sweet sherry. Of little interest to the connoisseur, but outsells all other sherries by a large margin.
Vintage Port	Made from very ripe grapes picked at 14 baume or more which are crushed and commence their fermentation like any red wine. Fortifying spirit (either so-called SVR at 95% or brandy spirit at 85%) is added at around 9 baume, producing a finished wine with an alcohol of around 3.5 to 5.5 baume of unfermented (or residual) sugar. The wine may be fortified on its skins (ie, in the fermenter) pressed and then fortified. The wine spends only a short time (less than one year) in barrel or tank before being bottled.	Shiraz, Grenache, Cabernet Sauvignon, Touriga	Hardy, Chateau Reynella, Seppelt	The Hardy and Reynella vintage ports stand supreme, but attract only limited interest. After a flurry of activity in the late seventies and early eighties triggered by a stamp-collecting label craze initiated by Yalumba with its racehorse series, the market for vintage port has all but disappeared. These wines deserve a better fate.
Tawny Port	Made in similar fashion to vintage port, but then aged in old, small barrels for decades, gradually changing colour from dark red to a pale glowing brown with no red tints whatsoever — hence the name tawny. Almost always a blend of many vintages.	Shiraz, Grenache, Mataro (or Mouvedre), Muscadelle	Seppelt, Lindemans, McWilliams, Yalumba, Penfolds, Saltram, Hardy, Orlando, Chateau Reynella	There are many styles (and qualities) grouped loosely under the tawny port banner, some with brand names (eg, Invalid, Royal Reserve). The cheapest wines are also the youngest, effectively a cross between vintage and tawny and are much heavier, fruitier and sweeter. True aged tawny ports have an almost ethereal elegance and delicacy, finishing dry after an intense, complex mid-palate.

FORTIFIED WINES

Type of Wine	Method of Making	Grapes Used	Direct Makers	General Comments
Muscat	Exceptionally ripe grapes (20 baume or even more in the greatest years) are crushed and fortified shortly after the commencement of fermentation; occasionally fortification takes place before fermentation commences. The secret of the greatest muscats lies in the use of very old wine (up to 60 years) to provide complexity, balanced by very young (5 years) material; blended with the major part which, according to quality, will be between 7 and 15 years of age.	Muscat a Petits Grains (or Brown Muscat or Brown Frontignac, as it is incorrectly called).	Morris, Bailey, Chambers, All Saints, Campbells, McWilliams, Seppelt, Stanton & Killeen, Bullers	Generally regarded as the greatest of the Australian fortified wines, and enjoying a renaissance in popularity among connoisseurs. The oldest have an unequalled concentration and intensity of flavour, explosively rich and sweet, but with balancing (and essential) acidity on the finish. To be consumed in very small glasses at the end of the meal, although younger (and less intense) muscat can be an excellent winter aperitif.
Tokay	Made in identical fashion to Muscat and – like Muscat – a specialty of North-east Victoria.	Muscadelle (often incorrectly called Tokay).	As above	Winemakers and wine judges often prefer tokay to muscat; the 'cold tea' aroma and taste is slightly less overtly sweet, although there is an equally great concentration of flavour in muscats and tokays of equivalent quality (and age).

LEFT: Pedro ximinez grapes at the end of spring flowering.

How they are made

Most fortified wines are made in a similar fashion: spirit with an alcohol content of between 60 and 95 per cent by volume is added to partially-fermented wine, lifting the average alcohol to between 17 and 19 per cent, thereby killing the yeasts and preventing any further fermentation. The wine is then transferred to barrel, and may spend many years there before being bottled.

The various types

The table opposite tells you about the main types, although in both sherry and port categories there are many sub-types and brand names which are not so easy to pigeon-hole — particularly in the lower-priced section of the market.

The alcohol question

Part of the reason for the decline in popularity of these wines stems from their perceived alcohol content and from the increasing discussion about health and social implications of alcohol in general. But you should remember that on average such wines contain only 50 per cent more alcohol than standard table wine (sometimes less), and that the glass normally used for fortified wines (the sherry glass) is about half size. In other words, a generous sherry glass will contain no more alcohol than a standard glass of table wine. The same applies to port, muscat and tokay.

The special attributes of fortified wine

With the exception of vintage ports, these wines have two advantages over table wines. Once bottled, they do not need further ageing: indeed, they will not improve or change once bottled. Second, they will last for months — years even — after they have been opened. So you can have a glass when the mood takes you, which makes a bottle a highly economical purchase. (A vintage port does improve with age in bottle, and will only last a day or two after it is opened.)

14 READING THE LABEL

'A glimpse of the label is worth thirty years experience in the wine trade.'
MICHAEL BROADBENT, LONDON

What ought to be a simple matter is in fact exceptionally difficult, for it is not only a question of understanding what the label does say but also what it does not say; of realising that some terms have a precise legal meaning, others none at all; of appreciating that some pieces of information are required by law, and that others are purely discretionary; and of having the means to interpret some cryptic disclosures which a well-intentioned legislature has decided should be made, but which are unintelligible to the lay person.

Introduction

The legal framework was established in 1963 when the various States enacted Pure Foods Regulations and which are now effectively embodied in the Commonwealth Food Standards Code 1987. The five basic provisions of that legislation are as follows. If a wine is said to be made from a particular variety, it must contain at least 80 per cent of that variety. If it is said to be made from a blend of varieties, those varieties must be listed in descending order of volume. If the wine is claimed to come from a particular region, it must contain 80 per cent of the wine from that region, while if it is said to be a blend of regions, they too must be listed in descending order. Finally, if a vintage is claimed, 95 per cent of the wine must be from that vintage.

The legal requirements

There are several obvious shortcomings in the legislation. For a start, there is no requirement that the actual percentages be specified, so a 'Shiraz Cabernet' may contain 55 per cent Shiraz and 45 per cent Cabernet Sauvignon, but equally well may be 95 per cent Shiraz and 5 per cent Cabernet Sauvignon. Next, the 80 per cent rule has a 'double-up' effect: a wine labelled Coonawarra Cabernet Sauvignon will comply with the regulations if it contains 60 per cent Coonawarra Cabernet Sauvignon, 20 per cent Coonawarra Shiraz, and 20 per cent Southern Vales Cabernet Sauvignon. Finally, the regulations presently do not seek to control the use of terms which in fact have no meaning.

The gaps and shortcomings

A modest start has been made on circumscribing the use of meaningless terms on labels, spurred on by the requirements of the European Economic Community (EEC), which dictates that 'descriptive terms' may only be used if they are prescribed by the producing country and approved by the EEC. The committee of the

Meaningless label jargon

101

A LABEL WHICH DISCLOSES REGION OF ORIGIN, GRAPE VARIETY AND VINTAGE

OPTIONAL INFORMATION

COMPULSORY INFORMATION OR OPTIONAL INFORMATION WITH LEGAL MEANING

Simply an indication of Murray Tyrrell's personal views of the quality of the wine; has no particular meaning.

In the dim distant past may have referred to a particular cask or vat; now simply akin to a brand name which should indicate a particular style which continues from year to year. Bin numbers fulfil the same role eg Penfolds Bin 389.

A traditional term with no particular meaning; in future vintages of this wine the grape variety (Hermitage, or Shiraz) will be specified in lieu of 'Dry Red', in which case 80 per cent of the wine must come from this variety.

Estate bottled has the common sense meaning, but is a purely optional statement in Australia.

The sort of description which often appears on the back label; while optional, the Trade Practices Act requires that nothing false or misleading is contained in it and the wine must contain 80 per cent Hermitage grapes.

Almost all table wines in fact bear a vintage date, but are not required to by law. If the vintage is stated, 95 per cent of the wine must have been vintaged from grapes grown in that year.

Brand name which may or may not be associated with the name of the producer.

Region of origin: no requirement for disclosure, but if stated, 80 per cent of the wine must have been made from grapes grown in that region.

Maker's name and address; mandatory unless bottling code is used.

The alcoholic content, which may be rounded off to the nearest half degree.

220 is the numeric code for sulphur dioxide, universally used in making both white and red wine. With white wines you will usually find the statement 'Antioxidant (300) added', referring to ascorbic acid (essentially Vitamin C) used in conjunction with sulphur dioxide.

Nett contents: a half bottle is 375ml, a magnum 1.5 litres.

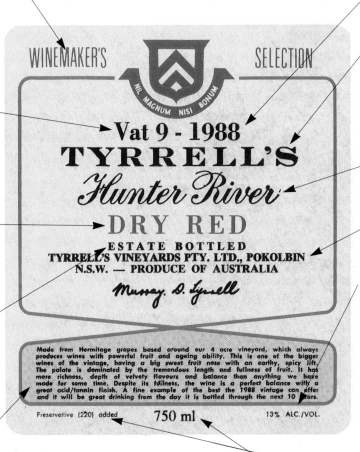

WINEMAKER'S SELECTION

NIL MAGNUM NISI BONUM

Vat 9 - 1988
TYRRELL'S
Hunter River
DRY RED
ESTATE BOTTLED
TYRRELL'S VINEYARDS PTY. LTD., POKOLBIN
N.S.W. — PRODUCE OF AUSTRALIA

Murray. D. Tyrrell

Made from Hermitage grapes based around our 4 acre vineyard, which always produces wines with powerful fruit and ageing ability. This is one of the bigger wines of the vintage, having a big sweet fruit nose with an earthy, spicy lift. The palate is dominated by the tremendous length and fullness of fruit. It has more richness, depth of velvety flavours and balance than anything we have made for some time. Despite its fullness, the wine is a perfect balance with a great acid/tannin finish. A fine example of the best the 1988 vintage can offer and it will be great drinking from the day it is bottled through the next 10 years.

Preservative (220) added   750 ml   13% ALC./VOL.

A LABEL WHICH MAKES NO CLAIMS OF REGION OF ORIGIN OR GRAPE VARIETY

The trading name of the winery but in fact not essential; for example, look at the label of Jamiesons Run. The only legal requirement is the name and address of the producer as given here.

The only mandatory information missing is the statement of additives, which will be found on the back label (not reproduced).

A brand name with no claim as to the grape varieties used, although the back label tells you they are in fact Shiraz, Malbec and Cabernet Sauvignon.

There is no claim that the wine comes from the Hunter Valley, or any other region. The name and address of the producer is required by law, and is not in fact any indication of the place of origin.

Australian Wine and Brandy Corporation has recommended that some descriptive terms be supported (under strict conditions) and that others be not supported. Those terms considered meaningless include 'Vintage Reserve', 'Special Vintage', 'Specially Selected', 'Exceptional' and 'Superior'. The committee suggests 'Winemaker's Selection' can only be used when the specific reason for its selection is specified on the label; 'Traditional' can be used only when none of the modern techniques of winemaking have been used in making the wine; 'Estate' must connote wine grown and produced (though not necessarily bottled) on the property described; and 'Show Reserve' can be used only for specific parcels of wine actually held for shows and ultimately released for sale.

Label Integrity Programme

In conjunction with these initiatives the Wine and Brandy Corporation (the Australian wine industry statutory body) has implemented the Label Integrity Programme (LIP). The laws have been in place since 1963; what has been lacking has been any effective enforcement or check procedures, simply because of lack of staff and funds. LIP has changed all that, and has already carried out major audits of all Clare Valley Rhine Riesling producers and all Hunter Valley Semillon producers. It has also carried out audits of particular makers, and will continue both broad-based and specific audits to ensure that any claim made on the label is accurate in all respects.

15 PURCHASING WINE

'I wonder often what the vinters buy one-half so precious as the stuff they sell.' OMAR KHAYAM

As you become more and more familiar with wine, your taste will change. Indeed, no matter how long you live and how experienced you become, that process of evolution will continue. It will be sustained by many things: your own increasing familiarity with wine in general; your exposure to hitherto unknown wines, most typically the great wines of France and the other European countries; by the changes in lifestyle as you grow older and — with luck — more affluent; and by the realisation that quality is better than quantity as you find the after-effects of excessive consumption are progressively more difficult to handle.

Introduction: your changing palate

But these are all changes from within, as it were. At the same time as you are maturing and changing, so are the wines you are buying. And here I am not talking about the sometimes unexpected changes which occur as the wine matures in bottle (explained in Chapter 17) but the changes in winemaking and wine style. Over the past twenty years there has been a flood of new grape varieties and an explosion in the viticultural map. New oak, once a luxury known only to a minority of winemakers, is now an essential part of premium winemaking. Winemakers have gone, and are continuing to go, through a steep learning curve, necessarily taking consumers along for the ride in the process.

Changes in wine style

So the first rule for the inexperienced buyer is to be very cautious. Indeed, it is a rule which also applies in some respects to the expert: wherever possible, taste the wine before buying any quantity. This may either involve the purchase of a single bottle, or possibly attending the in-store tastings which are frequently held by the fine wine retailers in most of the capital cities.

The first rule: be cautious

Next, collect as many expert opinions as you can on the wine. These will appear in books, newspapers, wine magazines and in wine club and retailer newsletters. Word of mouth recommendation may be reliable, but it may not. The advice of the retailer falls into the same category: if you build up a relationship with a good retailer who comes to understand your palate and personal style preference, that advice will be the best of all. At the other extreme is the retailer who has no real idea about your palate, but who has a vested interest in (that is large stocks of) a particular wine, and who is simply looking for a sale.

Expert opinion — valuable but not conclusive

For what you must remember is that while an expert can tell you whether a wine is very good, good or poor, that expert cannot tell you

Personal taste: for you alone to decide

whether or not you will (or should) like the wine. That is a purely personal and largely subjective decision. All one can say is that if you like the wine and the expert says it is very good, buy it with confidence. If you like the wine, but the expert says it is poor, be very careful: buy a bottle at a time, and be absolutely sure you still find the wine enjoyable.

RIGHT: The cellar door — these days not always the cheapest source, but by far the most fun.

Buying wine from discount retailers

If you live in one of the capital cities of the southern States (in other words, any city other than Brisbane and Darwin) retail shops offer the best all-round opportunity for buying the best wine at a fair price. Here, though, there is a choice: there are the aggressive discount retailers and chains which sell selected wines at the lowest possible price — sometimes below cost. Forget personalised, skilled advice: this is lowest common denominator selling, based at best on volume, and otherwise on loss-leader techniques. In other words, the retailer attracts customers by advertising selected wines at or below cost, while the remaining wines will be offered at a more normal price. What is more, the range of wines will inevitably concentrate on the high-volume, brand leaders.

The specialist fine wine retailer

The other choice is to set up a relationship with one or two fine wine specialist retailers. Unless and until Australia moves back into a full-scale boom after its 1991 recession, market-place competition will mean that you will be able to buy wine at a competitive price, even if not at the ultra-low price of the discounter. The compensation will be the expert advice and the range of good quality wines which the retailer has selected in the first instance: the retailer has in effect 'put his money where his mouth is', choosing wines which in his or her expert opinion represent the best available value for money. For no retailer in the country carries more than a modest selection of all of the thousands of different wines which the 650 or so wine producers in Australia have on sale at any one time.

Most of the credit card providers, several of the major retail stores (David Jones in particular), and a number of other organisations (most notably the non-profit Australian Wine Society) provide mail-order sales, with regular catalogues and standing pre-selected wine ordering systems. Those run by the credit cards are the most sophisticated, with the Cellarmasters organisation (which initiated the American Express Wine Cellar, but is no longer involved with it) operating one of the most highly developed, computerised systems in the world. These offer the country purchaser the opportunity of buying wine at city prices (or better), with the knowledge that a great deal of effort and expertise has gone into the selection of the wines in the first place. The principal drawback is the inevitably limited range of wines on offer, but for the beginner this can be a positive advantage, for it vastly simplifies choice.

Indeed, this simplicity and convenience of choice also brings the clubs and direct mail organisations substantial business from city-based clientele. Simply because there are so many wines and so many brands to choose from, buying wine can be an unnerving experience. Quite reasonably, the purchaser is afraid of appearing ignorant and of making the wrong choice. Other busy executives simply don't have the time to do personal shopping, least of all for the board room. Telling the personal secretary to order wine from the mail order offers which come with the credit card statement is a potent form of convenience shopping.

At the other extreme are the wine auctions, run by Langton's in Sydney and Melbourne and by Colin Gaetjens in Adelaide. These can be a happy hunting ground for collectors looking for the finest and rarest wines, but also for those simply seeking bargains. The auctions all offer a mail- or fax-bidding service, so there is no need to attend the auction if the time or location is inconvenient. Absentee bids have a second advantage: they eliminate the blood-lust fever which leads competing bidders at a live auction to push prices way above reasonable levels in the heat of the battle.

But there are traps. If you are bidding for old wines, it is essential that you or someone you trust physically inspect the bottles. The expert eye can often pick up signs of poor storage which may well have damaged the wine; in some instances even young wines will show such symptoms (principally a small stain or leak from the cork running down one side of the bottle). Ardent auction watchers will also track wines purchased at one auction and later resold, but with one bottle missing: the conclusion will be that the vendor was disappointed with his purchase. But there is no point in asking the auctioneer who is selling the wine and why: the identity of the seller and the motive for sale are closely-guarded secrets.

Auctions are the only legal means for an individual to sell wine, unless he or she is dead or bankrupt (or both). And even in these melancholy situations, the auction may be the most expedient method of selling substantial quantities of wine within a reasonably short time frame. So

Wine clubs and the country wine buyer

The intimidation factor

Auctions

The traps

The only way to sell wine

107

it by no means follows that the only wines sold at auction are unwanted orphans: some of the greatest wines — both Australian and imported — are only to be found at auction.

The cellar door

Finally, there is the winery cellar door (supplemented by the mailing list which most of the small wineries operate). For many, going to the winery to taste and buy the wine is the most enjoyable method. The Australian wine districts are extremely varied in their scenery and in the feel of the wineries, but I cannot think of one which does not have its own special beauty. All of the capital cities have at least one wine district within a few hours drive, Melbourne and Adelaide being particularly fortunate.

A privilege not a right

In almost all instances, the wine tasting is free, and in most regions several of the wineries have on-site restaurants. Tasting facilities are positively luxurious compared to those I encountered when I first started visiting wineries, as is the choice of wineries to visit. You are not necessarily expected to buy wine, but on the other side of the coin, remember the cost to the wine producer. Not only is he or she giving the tasting wine away, but is paying 20 per cent sales tax to the Federal Government for the privilege of so doing. On top of this there is the capital cost of the tasting facility, the cost of glasses (which get broken and which disappear) and the cost of wages for the support staff. Free tastings like this are a privilege which should not be abused.

16 STARTING A CELLAR

'Forget the house, forget the children, I want custody of the red and access to the port once a month.'
KEVIN CHILDS

If Michael Broadbent and Professor Emile Peynaud have managed to write books on wine tasting, so have I managed to write a book on the subject of starting a cellar: *Setting Up Your Own Wine Cellar*, also published by Angus and Robertson. Thus this chapter is the briefest possible introduction to what is once again a subject which merits a book in its own right.

There are two distinct sides to the subject: the cellar itself, and what to put in it. But before I go any further, let me freely admit that theory and reality may be quite different. I well remember my first cellar and how proud I was of it: it was the linen cupboard in my fifth storey flat which — by the time I could fit no more in it — held just under 300 bottles, a number which my friends (and I secretly) regarded as quite remarkable. In fact it is just as well it did not hold more, for it was far from ideal storage. Which, I suppose, is as good a lead-in as any to the requirements of a good, medium- to long-term cellar.

By far the most important aspect is protection against diurnal (day/night) temperature fluctuations. If this is achieved, the other features will either follow automatically, or can be achieved with a minimum of difficulty and expense. What is a maximum acceptable daily fluctuation? Well, 0.1 degree Celsius (32 degrees Fahrenheit) would be perfect, 5 degrees Celsius (41 degrees Fahrenheit) would be excessive, 10 degrees Celsius (50 degrees Fahrenheit) not far removed from ambient or external fluctuations and utterly unacceptable. It may seem surprisingly stringent, but anything over a 1 degree Celsius (33.8 degrees Fahrenheit) daily fluctuation means you should either give up the idea of storing wine for more than a year or two, find another cellar spot, or fix up the deficiencies in the one you have.

For extending the daily variation out to seasonal fluctuation, once you go above 1 degree Celsius (33.8 degrees Fahrenheit) on a daily basis you are headed above a 10 degree Celsius (50 degrees Fahrenheit) winter/summer range, compared with a realistically acceptable variation of 7 to 9 degrees Celsius (44.6 to 48.2 degrees Fahrenheit) and a target of 2 to 3 degrees Celsius (35.6 to 37.4 degrees Fahrenheit).

The only way to know what is going on in the cellar is to install a double-bulb thermometer, which records both minimum and maximum temperatures over any given period (a reset button returns the system to start again). So many people I have spoken to tell me

Introduction

The requirements of the cellar

Daily temperature fluctuation

Winter/summer fluctuation

The only reliable measure — a thermometer

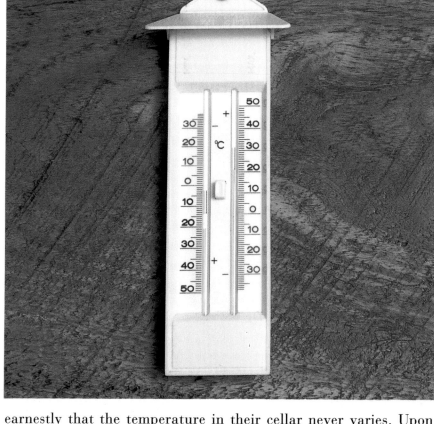

earnestly that the temperature in their cellar never varies. Upon questioning, they admit they do not have a thermometer — least of all a double-bulb thermometer — and base their assertion upon the proposition that it is always cool in summer when they walk in.

The reality

Well, for a start it should also feel warm in winter when they walk in. For another, I refer them to a cellar I had built under my then house at Turramurra, one of Sydney's northern suburbs. It was excavated out of sandstone, was entirely underground, and had a concrete slab as its roof which was the ground floor of a split three-level house. Yet its year-round temperature varied by 9 degrees Celsius (48.2 degrees Fahrenheit), simply reflecting the change in ground temperature to a depth of 304 cm (10 feet).

Suffice to say that if you live in Brisbane, Perth or Sydney, finding a naturally cool and temperature-stable cellar under or in your house is impossible; in Melbourne and Adelaide it will be very difficult, although the massive bluestone houses of Adelaide offer some hope. So one descends from the ideal to the less than ideal, and the question is what to do about it.

Insulation and air-conditioning — ideal but expensive

Insulation supplemented by a dedicated air conditioner-humidifier will give a perfect result, but is very expensive and appropriate only for the wealthy, serious collector. In a more real world, you should try to find a spot under the house which is entirely enclosed and thus protected from both draughts and light; failing this, a centrally-located room or cupboard.

Cardboard cartons

Once you come down to this level, try to resist the temptation of having your bottles 'on display'. The cardboard cartons in which wines are packed are efficient insulators, and also protect the wine from light. Their downsides are, it is true, numerous: tendency to collapse in humid or wet environments, and difficulty of access, particularly when stacked one on the other, being the most obvious.

The styrene 'Cellar Box'

An expensive alternative, but one which becomes essential in tropical climates if an air-conditioned room is not available, are specially designed styrene boxes which double up as wine racks and nearly perfect insulation. They stack on their sides, with individual holes for each bottle, and with lids which can be removed even when the boxes are stacked several high. The principal version is Cellar Box, manufactured in Melbourne by Mr Tony Jackson (phone (03) 692 7226).

Racking systems

Which brings me to racking or storage systems within the cellar. If you have a temperature-stable environment, open or display storage becomes viable. The systems are numerous, ranging from wooden banana boxes stored on their sides through to custom-built wooden or metal individual bottle storage racks, which I describe and illustrate at some length in *Setting Up Your Own Wine Cellar*. If you do not have such an environment, then the cardboard wine carton will help, the styrene box will work miracles.

What to put in the cellar

I have already warned you about the trebly-shifting sands of time; in other words, pointed out that not only will the wine in your cellar change as it ages, and not only will your own palate change, but so will winemaking techniques and philosophies, resulting in a change in the style (and very possibly quality) of the current or future vintage wines.

The pitfalls

The result has been a bitter pill (or bitter wine) for many a novice collector. He or she pulls out a bottle of wine jealously hoarded for three or four years, presents it with infinite pride at the special dinner party, and is absolutely mortified: the wine is flat, dull and uninteresting, at best passing without notice or comment, at worst greeted with embarrassed silence if the host has been unwise enough to announce its arrival with a fanfare of trumpets.

How to avoid the pitfalls

First and foremost, do not cellar cheap wine in the fond hope that time will turn a sour's ear into a silk purse. Conversely, the more expensive a wine is, the more likely it is to repay cellaring. So the first law is to drink the cheap wine, and cellar the finest. Exceptions will prove this rule just as much as any other, and if an expert who you really trust recommends a cheap wine for the cellar, by all means have a long-odds punt, but do not expect a 100 per cent success rate.

Buy in reasonable quantities

If you are going to seriously cellar a wine, buy it in a reasonable quantity: not less than six bottles, and preferably one to two dozen bottles. Space and economics may prevent this, but the consequence is that your collection will be a haphazard and largely accidental one, a convenient storehouse upon which to draw but no more than that.

If you are able to follow my advice, try a bottle every six or twelve months. If the wine tastes wonderful, drink it up and be happy. Do not make the mistake I used to fall prey to of saying to yourself 'This is fantastic; I must hold onto it' — one cannot improve on what seems to be perfection.

Taste regularly

It may seem trite to say that a cellar should be balanced, but it is surprising how many people only consider cellaring red wines (and possibly fortified wines). White wines can be every bit as rewarding, if not more so, if only because of the surprise factor. Elsewhere in this book I suggest the types of wines which will repay cellaring: suffice it to say here that a fifteen to twenty-year-old Semillon or Rhine Riesling can be a magnificent wine of world class.

A balanced cellar

But do not force the issue. Understanding and enjoying fully mature wine is something which will only come with experience. For the beginner such a wine may be wasted at best, or unpleasant at worst. What is more, even the most dedicated collector and connoisseur will not wish to drink old wine all the time. There will always be occasions when the untamed exuberance of a young wine at the start of its life is what is required.

Be your own judge

ABOVE: ARC weldmesh offers single bottle storage at the most economical price in the larger cellar.

113

RIGHT: *Wines can be sorted by region, by maker, by vintage or by variety — or a combination.*

The signs of trouble in the cellar

It remains to warn briefly of the signs that all is not well in your cellar. If you follow the advice of reasonably regular tasting, your palate (and the judgement of those with whom you share the bottle) should with luck give you warning. But there are also physical signs, by far the most important being the development of ullage, or airspace between the bottom of the cork and the level of the wine when you stand the bottle upright. It is a subject which I explain at some length in *Setting Up Your Own Wine Cellar* (and also how to deal with the problem).

A fatal disease

Many people are born collectors, whether it be stamps, coins, cereal cards, dolls, paintings, painted eggs or anything else under the sun. The same disease affects wine drinkers; one only has to read magazines such as America's *Wine Spectator* to be amazed at the obsession which collecting wine can become. Some would say that I have been bitten by the same bug, but I would answer by saying there is one difference. I collect wine with the intention of drinking it, and for no other purpose. When visitors look at a very old and rare bottle in my cellar and say 'But how could you ever bear to drink it?' my response is 'How can I bear not to drink it'. Remember that whenever you take a special bottle from your cellar for the special dinner party, it costs you nothing. It only cost you money to put it into the cellar.

17 HOW AND WHY A WINE AGES

'Wine lives and dies; it has not only its hot youth, strong maturity and weary dotage, but also its seasonal changes, its mysterious, almost mystical, link with its parent vine, so that when the sap is running in the wood on the middle slopes of the Côte d'Or, in a thousand cellars a thousand miles away, the wine in its bottle quickens and responds.' EVELYN WAUGH 1937

Introduction

This is the most technical and difficult chapter in the book, yet it deals with the subject which all wine drinkers find the most fascinating, so I guess it had to be written. It may well be the one chapter which you will wish to re-read in the years to come, and if so, it will have served its purpose (however belatedly). For this and other reasons, I will use some daunting technical terminology and involve you in a certain amount of biochemistry.

When will this wine be at its best?

For if you are ever to answer for yourself the inevitable question 'When will this wine be at its best?' you will need to understand at least some of the things I deal with here. At the outset you should realise that all correctly made and bottled wines undergo certain inevitable and basic changes from the moment the cork goes into place on the bottling line. Reduced to ultimate simplicity, a wine will progressively lose fruit aroma and taste (as we have seen earlier, described as primary and secondary aromas and tastes) while simultaneously gaining in complexity. Obviously enough, there finally comes a point at which there is no more complexity to gain, and another point at which there is no more fruit to lose. Somewhere between these points, or after the second point to occur, the wine will start to decline and eventually decay.

The maturity graph

In its simplest form, this means the ageing potential of a wine can be expressed in the form of a graph (see page 116) with a shaded area around the point at which the lines cross. This shaded area simply reflects the fact that a wine does not reach the peak of its development on one day, and start to decline the next. Depending on how long it has taken to reach its peak, it will enter a plateau phase during which it neither improves nor declines. The more rapidly it reaches its plateau, the shorter will be the plateau, and the quicker its decline (with the converse holding true).

ABOVE: The cellars of Thomas Hardy contain gems dating back to last century.

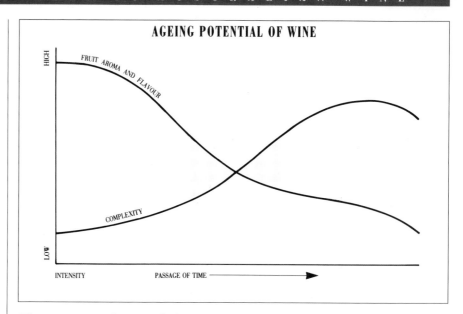

AGEING POTENTIAL OF WINE

The most subjective judgement of all

The neat simplicity of the graph is nonetheless challenged by an unquantifiable factor: how much weight and importance do you place on fruit flavour and freshness, and how much importance do you place on complexity? There is no right or wrong in this: it is a purely personal, subjective decision. What is more, it is a decision which will almost certainly change as you become more familiar with wine, and gradually place more weight on complexity, less on primary fruit.

The basic chemical changes

Now to the more difficult matter of chemistry. The most important process of change involves the interaction of the small quantity of dissolved oxygen (present in all young wine) with the tannins, anthocyanins, flavones, and the various acids present in the wine. The changes are technically known as reductive (or reducing), because they progressively reduce the potential for further change by utilising all the available oxygen. (If the cork fails, and fresh oxygen enters the bottle, the changes will be both rapid and destructive.)

The changes in red wine: polymerisation

The changes in red wine are not only the most easily observed, but are far better understood than those which occur with white wine. They fall into two main categories: polymerisation and esterification. Polymerisation is caused by the action of oxygen on the tannins and anthocyanins (which are coloured forms of tannin) and leads to the progressive change in the colour of a red wine from the vivid purple-red of youth to the dark red of middle age and finally the pale brick or tawny red of old age. This is triggered by the progressive aggregation of the anthocyanins and tannins which first form a fine sediment and ultimately a crust or deposit which collects on the sides of the bottle. A concurrent but invisible change is the softening of the flavour and structure of the tannins as they, too, polymerise.

Esterification

The other principal change is esterification: it too involves the interaction of oxygen, this time with acids and alcohol to form esters and aldehydes. There is some disagreement between the experts on the extent to which these changes impact on the development of the bouquet, although pragmatic experience clearly suggests there is a

LEFT: A selection of vintage wines from the cellars of Yalumba.

profound influence. The disagreement stems not so much from the facts of the changes, but how those changes affect what we smell and taste — and how the interaction of the compounds may alter the taste and smell of one taken in isolation. Incidentally, esterification does not reduce the acidity of the wine: contrary to widely held belief, acidity does not diminish (in chemical terms) as a wine ages. What happens is that the acid appears to soften as a wine reaches its peak due to the increased complexity of the other flavour compounds.

White wine ageing: colour

As I have said elsewhere, no one claims to have unlocked the process by which a well-made white wine changes from a light green-straw in its youth to a glowing buttercup or golden yellow, still tinged with green, at full maturity five to twenty years later. The colour of the best of such wines is truly remarkable, seemingly lit by a light from within. The source is thought to be a flavone (or flavonoid) which is a yellow pigment found in the skin of the grape. The problem is that while an Australian Chardonnay made with extended skin contact may have a significant level of flavones, a Rhine Riesling will have only trace quantities in the juice and the finished wine. Other variables come from Gewurztraminer and Muscat, which may pick up a pink tinge from their skins; yet another is the brown tinge which affects an oxidised or madeirised white wine which is insufficiently protected by sulphur dioxide, and which is a sure sign of unwelcome decay.

Aroma

Because most Australian white wines (those made by the major companies and those by the best-equipped small wineries) are fermented at low temperatures using specially selected yeasts, and are rigorously protected from oxidation once fermentation is finished, they tend to show a far more pronounced yeast and fruit aroma early in their life than their European counterparts. This may manifest itself as a tropical fruit through to grapefruit accent (generally regarded as attractive, though not by all makers), but may also give rise to a rather sweaty, closed aroma which I describe as armpit or armpit-like.

As the wine matures in bottle, the exotic fruit aromas will diminish and the sweaty character should disappear — in both instances fairly quickly. The true varietal aroma of the grape will show itself, and any prickle of sulphur dioxide present at bottling will diminish. Depending on the variety, a toasty, nutty or honeyed bouquet (all associated with a softening of the secondary fruit aroma and sometimes a blurring of the varietal fruit character) will build.

Taste

The changes basically reflect those of the bouquet. From the exotic, exuberant and tingling freshness of sometimes undisciplined youth, the wine becomes more harmonious and soft as it matures, progressively becoming richer and more honeyed before plateauing and eventually losing the sweet fruit it once had — or drying out, as the saying goes. These changes, incidentally, are as evident in the feel of the wine in the mouth as they are in terms of pure flavour.

Red wine: colour

The progressive lightening in the density of the colour, linked with the changes in hue, have already been explained. Suffice it to say here that there tends to be an excessive emphasis placed on both density and youthful purple colour in Australia: a mature wine can be quite light in colour, as long as it is bright, clear and alive.

Aroma

The smell of a six-month-old and as yet unbottled Cabernet Sauvignon destined to live for twenty years or more is not for the faint-hearted or the uninitiated. It has all the raw untamed power of a thoroughbred horse before it has been broken in; judging such wines in wine shows is a generally thankless task. But as the carbon dioxide dissolved in the wine during the primary fermentation and in the subsequent malolactic fermentation escapes, it takes with it some of the harsher and more bitter volatile aromas present in the young wine. The other changes are those associated with polymerisation and esterification, which help soften and round the aroma. These changes continue (albeit more slowly) once the wine is bottled: because there are more aroma and flavour-forming substances in red wine than in white, the extent of the changes is more dramatic, and the potential for complexity so much greater.

Taste

The causes of the changes in taste are the same as those which operate on the bouquet. As the tannins and anthocyanins are polymerised, and the esters and aldehydes are formed, the usually raw and rather harsh fruit of a young red wine gives way to a soft, gently sweet fruit flavour, gradually acquiring a gently earthy taste. The tannins, too, will soften; the mouth-puckering astringency of youth will ultimately become velvety smooth.

The intense sappy strawberry-plum fruit of a young Pinot, the striking pepper-spice of a young Shiraz, the amalgam of blackcurrant and capsicum of a young Cabernet will respectively soften as secondary and tertiary cedary-tobacco nuances start to manifest themselves. It is in learning about these changes, and deciding for yourself where you wish to draw the line, that so much of the excitement of wine lies.

ABOVE: The Tintara brand name can be traced back to the mid-nineteenth century.

18 SERVING WINE

'Gentlemen, pray be seated. The wine is at your elbows and your carriages within a hiccup's call.'
LA MARQUISE DE BRINVILLIERS

Introduction

It is perfectly possible to make the whole business of serving, tasting and assessing wine a deadly serious affair. If you are a group of dedicated oenophiles, with a collective experience of 100 years' wine tasting and are opening a century-old First Growth Bordeaux red, that seriousness may be warranted. But for the beginner, and in the ordinary run of day to day life, the less pretension, the better. As I stress in the next chapter, rules are there to be broken, and wine should never be elevated above its true purpose: to provide pleasure. More than anything else, it should not be allowed to intimidate anyone. So the suggestions which follow are simply that: a guide to be followed if you are unsure what to do, and to be discarded as soon as you gain the assurance to form your own judgement.

Glasses — an all-important choice

The choice of glassware is in part a functional decision, and in part an aesthetic one. No one has proved this better than the Austrian glassmaker Georg Riedel, who regularly conducts wine tastings — or should I say glass tastings — around the world proving the dramatic influence the size and shape of a glass has on the aroma and taste of a given wine. He typically selects a classic dry white, a light-bodied red wine, a full-bodied dry red, and a sweet white wine. Each wine is poured into, say, four differently-shaped glasses, and the wine is then smelt and tasted from each glass. Having read wine magazine reports, and having myself participated in such a tasting (in Japan, of all places) I can vouch for the fact that the differences are quite extraordinary. You can in fact run a small experiment yourself without a battery of exquisite but expensive crystal glasses. Simply pour a good red wine into the finest and thinnest tasting glass (preferably the International Standards Organisation (ISO) glass illustrated opposite), and also pour the same wine into a heavy glass milk or beer tumbler. Even the most inexperienced taster will be able to perceive the difference; indeed, unless the taster is told the wine in the two glasses is the same, he or she will be sure there is a different wine in each glass.

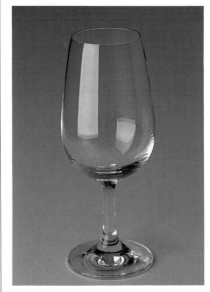

ABOVE: The ISO wine glass.

The glasses themselves

I have a personal preference for simple glasses made from fine crystal; Orrefors and Riedel make the best available. A selection is shown in the photograph with two special glasses included, the ISO tasting glass and the Impitoyable. The ISO glass is the best multi-purpose glass available: there are two basic sources, China and Austria. The Chinese glasses are the cheapest, but are heavy and sometimes slightly discoloured. The Impitoyable is an extremely ugly glass which

massively concentrates — some say distorts — the bouquet, as vigorous swirling of the thin layer of wine with its very large surface area aids the liberation of volatile aromas. Impitoyable, incidentally, means The Merciless One.

The importance of ambient temperature

It has always seemed to me that precise temperature guides for serving wine are less than useful. Putting a thermometer in your guest's wine glass is not likely to impress: you should *know* the temperature is correct. What is more, the temperature at which the wine should be served will be heavily influenced by the ambient temperature. On a hot summer's day, white wines should be served fully chilled (that is refrigerator temperature) and then kept in an ice bucket or insulated wine cooler. Conversely, red wine should either be slightly chilled or kept in the cellar until the last possible moment. The reason in each case is that wine in a glass rapidly responds to temperature differential, and there is nothing worse than blood warm red wine on a hot summer's day unless it be tepid white wine.

Serving temperatures

ABOVE: From left to right: sparkling wine, aromatic dry white, full-bodied white, light-bodied dry red, full-bodied dry red, sweet white.

If the ambient temperature is around 20 degrees Celsius (68 degrees Fahrenheit), that differential becomes much less important, and broad guidelines apply. Sparkling and sweet wine should be served cold, that is fully chilled; the fuller bodied the dry white wine, the warmer it may be, although it is best slightly chilled; light-bodied red wines can be served at roughly the same temperature (that is very slightly chilled or straight from the cellar); while full-bodied red wines are fine at room temperature.

LEFT: *A candle is the most romantic method, but a torch does the job of pinpointing the sediment just as well.*

Much controversy exists about the practice of drawing the cork early to allow the wine to breathe, and even more so about the time lapse between decanting and service. Some fairly complicated chemistry is involved in understanding the causes of the changes which take place (basically involving a rapid acceleration of some of the chemistry of ageing) and it is sufficient here to understand the end result.

Breathing and decanting wine

In general terms, the older the wine, the more rapid and the more marked will be the changes. After thirty years of indecision, I have finally come to subscribe to the school of thought which says 'You can wait for the wine, but the wine will not wait for you.' In other words, old wines should be uncorked and decanted no more than half an hour before service. The younger and more robust the wine, the less responsive it is, and the more elastic the time frame, although I have often wondered what the point of decanting young wine is (other than a useful habit to get into if you plan to drink older wine from time to time).

The time frames

Simply drawing the cork is the most gentle method of commencing the breathing process, and even an old wine will react slowly to it. Decant the wine, and the situation changes dramatically, as fresh oxygen is absorbed by the wine at a far more rapid rate. The immediate change will (hopefully) be the disappearance of any so-called 'bottle stink', a slightly musty, mushroomy, stale smell which sometimes can be detected as an old wine is first opened. If, however, the wine is corked or oxidised, the sour, bitter smell will not disappear, but will indeed

The effect of breathing

intensify. The next change in a sound wine will be the evolution of its true bouquet, which will initially intensify but ultimately fade and collapse, perhaps having undergone several changes along the way.

Decanting

Decanting serves two purposes: to accelerate the breathing process (coupled with the second defacto decanting as the wine is poured into the glass) and to leave any sediment or crust in the bottle. It is most commonly employed for red wines, but old, full-bodied white wines (particularly French) can also need decanting. The result should be a star-bright wine in the glass.

Finally, whatever the shape of the glass, do not over-fill it: half to two thirds full is more than adequate.

19 WINE AND FOOD

'There are no rules about the drinking and serving of wine as might have been brought down by Moses...'
CYRIL RAY, *RAY ON WINE* (J. M. DENT, 1979)

It may seem trite, and a not terribly useful statement of the obvious, but only you can decide what combinations of wine and food please you most. There are no rights and wrongs in the choice, just a series of apparently endless permutations and combinations. There is no question, however, that there is a positive interaction between the taste of the wine and that of the food; sometimes it is pleasing, sometimes less so. Thus you should always try to taste the wine before the chosen food; you will be surprised how much the food will alter your perception of the taste of the wine.

Once you become thoroughly comfortable with wine, you will not dream of serving spirits, beer or mixed drinks before the meal, or certainly not before a formal dinner party. In time you will also realise there are many different wine types to choose from at this stage of the proceedings.

The most conventional is sparkling wine, the greatest being champagne (by which I mean French, and only that). I personally prefer the lighter, blanc de blancs styles, unless the dinner is a particularly serious one, in which case one might dig deep for an older vintage Bollinger or Krug — wines which are normally reserved for food. The classic accompaniment is caviar, but Parmigana Reggiano or King Island Surprise Bay Cheddar with Nashi Pear is also a brilliant match.

Introduction

BEFORE THE MEAL: APÉRITIF WINES

Sparkling wine

LEFT: Champagne accompanied by Victorian Parmesan is a superb apéritif.

Spatlese rieslings

A less conventional aperitif is a semi-sweet white wine, such as a spatlese riesling — either German or Australian. I find these wines are very difficult to match with food, unless it be something like prosciutto and melon, itself a simple and tasty hors d'oeuvre. The sweetness and fruitiness of these wines is perfect in itself, even if the style is much underrated and sadly neglected in consequence. Orlando and Leo Buring make some of the best spatlese rieslings, the older the better.

Sherry, tawny port, muscat and tokay

A fine fino or amontillado sherry is as classic an introduction to an evening meal as one could wish for. Sadly, sherry is regarded as old fashioned by younger wine drinkers, although for the older aficionados this is a boon: Seppelt's and Lindemans' top sherries can be bought for a fraction of their true worth. There are also some brilliant Spanish sherries (the Almenacistas of Emilio Lustau) regularly imported into Australia. These can be matched with almost any hors d'oeuvre, particularly if it has a bite — like anchovies.

Tawny port, muscat and tokay may raise eyebrows, but France is by far the largest market in the world for Portuguese tawny port, much of it consumed in bars or as an aperitif. In winter, I love a glass of muscat, tokay or oloroso sherry before a normal evening meal — in summer a chilled fino sherry.

BELOW: Yabbies from the dam on the vineyard which produced the Chardonnay — a combination made in heaven.

The obvious choice is a white wine, and the less obvious but potentially no less successful a choice light-bodied red wine, with Pinot Noir leading the way. One of the reasons for the tidal wave of Chardonnay which is sweeping the world is the flexibility of the wine: a mainstream one- to two-year-old Australian Chardonnay will sit happily with almost any dish one can imagine. Nonetheless, full-flavoured fish (particularly with cream sauces), chicken, veal or pasta-based dishes are grist to the Chardonnay mill.

Finer seafood dishes — oysters are the most obvious example — and salads (nicoise or similar) demand a finer flavour. Unwooded Sauvignon Blancs and young to medium-aged Semillons come into their own in this context. Australian chablis may or may not: theoretically it should, but winemakers have taken a cynical view about what ought to be put into a bottle bearing the name chablis.

Those who know and appreciate Rhine Riesling say that it offers the best of all worlds, covering all of the circumstances and foods I have so far discussed. They are right, and I would only add Asian food to the Rhine Riesling — and Gewurztraminer — repertoire. Traminer, in particular, comes into its own, its spicy flavour mirroring that of the food.

Likewise Pinot Noir can be amazingly synergistic with Asian dishes, particularly less spicy Chinese food, and most especially seafood. It is a superb match with cooked fresh salmon, even if game — quail, pigeon, venison and so forth — is the more usual counterpart. In the height of summer, I would lightly chill the Pinot Noir when served with any of these dishes. The wine I would never serve with fish is a full-bodied red wine: the fish seems to imbue the wine with a bitter, metallic taste.

All of the wine and food primers of days gone by emphasise the white wine with white meat, red wine with red meat rule — and as a bottom-line simplification, one cannot quarrel with it. The stronger the flavour and structure of the red wine, the stronger should be that of the food. What else could one possibly serve with a thick, rare, barbequed rump steak than a young, robust Cabernet Sauvignon or Shiraz? If you don't like red wine, have a beer — but do not expect a white wine to provide anything more than liquid balance, and above all do not waste a fine quality white wine with such a flavour powerhouse.

It also follows that there are some foods for which there is no vinous match. Full-blown Indian curries, strong Szechuan dishes, highly-spiced Thai and Korean meals — here green tea, iced water or beer (or all three) are a far more sensible match.

Within the vast choice of red meat dishes and red wines there are an infinite number of satisfying combinations. Many experienced wine drinkers — myself included — would prefer claret style wines (in other words Cabernet Sauvignon) with lamb and burgundy style (Shiraz and Pinot Noir) with game and dishes such as Boeuf Bourgignonne, Coq au Vin and so forth — leaving steak and roast beef as a multi-choice, multipurpose meat.

ENTRÉES AND LIGHT MEALS
Chardonnay

Semillon and Sauvignon Blanc

Rhine Riesling and Traminer: Asian food

Pinot Noir

THE MAIN COURSES
Full-bodied red wines

Beer, tea or water

The red meat choices

CHEESE

Cheese has long been seen (and rightly so) as the ideal foil for red wine, but life is never as simple as it may seem at first sight. For a start, do you serve the clarets before the burgundies (conventional wisdom) or vice versa (my personal choice)? Next, you will come to find there are some cheeses (Stilton and other strong blue types) which overwhelm almost all red wines, and are best left to do battle with vintage ports. The most sympathetic cheeses are the milder-flavoured cheeses — cheddar-styles — and soft, double creams such as Brie and Camembert.

The order of service

Which reminds me: if you are staging a full-scale dinner party, or doing the full bit in a restaurant, and are having both cheese and dessert, *always* have the cheese first. It accompanies the red wine (unless it be Stilton), and the sweet table wines go with the dessert — or, in the case of an old Chateau d'Yquem (the famous sauterne of Bordeaux), with either the cheese or the dessert (or both).

DESSERTS
Sweet table wines

Earlier in this chapter I said that the taste of wine was different before and after you have taken your first mouthful of food. Nowhere does that apply with greater force than with sweet table wines: before the first spoonful, the wine will seem very much sweeter and obviously luscious than after. Depending on the weight of the wine (and its true level of sweetness) this may or may not be a bad thing. But it does highlight two things: it is easy to overwhelm even the most majestic sweet wine (a Riesling Trockenbeerenauslese or a Semillon sauterne style), and secondly, it reinforces my view that spatlese-style Rieslings are better served at the start of the meal than the end.

Champagne or not

It is not uncommon to find champagne or Methode Champenoise sparkling wine served with dessert. The practice grew up in an era in which very sweet champagnes were common, sometimes called Cuvée Russe, attesting to the taste of the then-considerable Russian market. Why the practice should have remained in favour once sweet champagne disappeared is beyond me: great chefs can devise suitable desserts, but they are few and far between. It follows that a good quality Italian spumante can make a neat marriage, and an Australian variant only slightly less so, but not dry sparkling wines.

COFFEE AND PETITS FOURS
Muscat, tokay and port

While I have suggested the occasional glass of sweet fortified wine may not go astray at the start of the meal, such wines come into their own at the end, served with potent coffee and petits fours. North-east Victorian muscats and tokays are among our very greatest wines, and are almost a meal in themselves. Simply because they are consumed last they tend to be blamed for the hangover, which is most unfair. One should blame the first glass, which started it all, rather than the last. Vintage port is traditionally matched with cheese, walnuts and raisins: I prefer the last two, and would forego the cheese.

The finale

If the thirst is still with you, or the occasion an especially happy one, now is the turn of the 'palate-cleanser' of champagne (or dare I say beer) or the 'digestive', a fine cognac. Simply remember that the idea inevitably seems much better at the time than it does the following morning.

20 WINE AND HEALTH

'Drink no longer water, but use a little wine for thy stomach's sake and thine often infirmities.'
1 TIMOTHY, 5:23

Since biblical times, and over the centuries, philosophers, moralists and medical practitioners have all praised the beneficial effect of wine in moderation on the health of both the individual and of society. Much of this was based upon simple observation of the overt effects of moderate consumption; now modern scientific research enables us to understand why that observation (and that praise) was correct. The bottom line, as it were, is that the male who drinks four glasses of wine a day and the female who drinks two glasses of wine a day is less likely to die (from any cause) than the total abstainer or the alcohol abuser. But before I explain the basis and findings of that research let me use the common-sense (and perhaps cynical) approach of a former lawyer.

If one believed the dire warnings — propaganda is not too strong a word — of the assorted Jeremiahs who come together in an ungodly coalition against alcohol (and to them wine is no different to any other form of alcohol), civilisation as we know it today would not exist. Particularly in Western Europe, foetal abnormalities, cancer, cirrhosis and homicide (to mention but a few) should have long since decimated the population if the United States Surgeon General's wine-label warnings (and the enthusiastic echoes and distortions from countless others) are justified. Per capita wine consumption in Italy and France is ten times as great as it is in the United States, yet alcoholism in Italy is all but unknown, and France has no greater number of deformed children than any other country. Tell a French or Italian mother she should not drink wine during her pregnancies and she would give you a look of withering disbelief — yet their consumption is far greater than even the most relaxed physician in Australia would recommend.

The other general observation is that those who attack the consumption of alcohol in any circumstances or at any level conveniently ignore the critical difference between use and abuse. There are many essentials in our life which are dangerous if used recklessly or irresponsibly — the motor car being the most obvious — and alcohol (wine included) is no different. The most widely used rule in Australia for measuring responsible consumption is the National Health and Medical Research Council (NHMRC) recommendation of four glasses of wine a day for men and two for women, which in turn derives from a distillation of the worldwide research conducted over the past twenty five years.

Introduction

The neo-prohibitionist doomsdayers

Use and abuse

ABOVE: A 285 ml glass of beer, 120 ml glass of wine and 30 ml nip of whiskey — each contains 10 grams of alcohol.

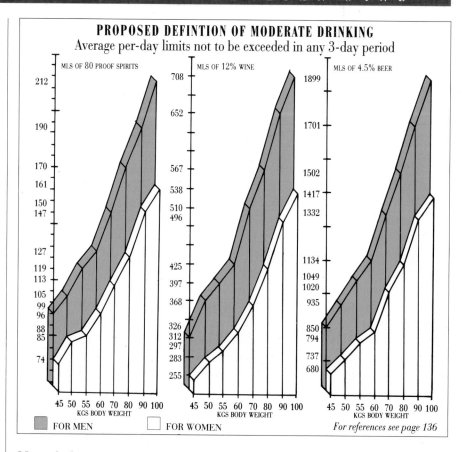

PROPOSED DEFINTION OF MODERATE DRINKING
Average per-day limits not to be exceeded in any 3-day period

FOR MEN ▢ FOR WOMEN *For references see page 136*

Pluses and minuses

Nonetheless, it is a generalisation, and suffers from the inevitable drawbacks of any such rule. On the downside, it is valid for healthy adults: it has no application for children, for drivers of motor cars, for those in ill-health or taking certain medications, and may be inappropriate for pregnant females. Nor does it take into account body weight (other than by the crude differentiation between males and females). Dr Thomas Turner of the John Hopkins University in the United States has devised a formula which suggests in each day you may safely drink that number of ounces of wine equal to your body weight in kilograms divided by four.

Units of measurement

One of the difficulties in all of this is the lack of any precise definition of what constitutes a glass of wine. The NHMRC guideline assumes a glass contains 120 ml (4.5 fl oz) of wine, which is in turn the equivalent of a 30 ml (1 fl oz) nip of spirits or a 285 ml (9.64 fl oz) glass of beer — in each case containing 10 grams of alcohol. The variables come from glass size (many hold rather more than 120 ml) and the alcohol level of the wine, which in Australia varies between 10 per cent and 14 per cent. Nonetheless, if you see reference to a unit of alcohol, it will be to one of the above standard equivalents.

How much wine do Australians in fact drink?

The most recent research (1989) conducted in Australia by McNair Anderson of consumption patterns of all forms of alcohol showed that only 1.2 per cent to 1.6 per cent of those who drink wine do so at levels exceeding the NHMRC recommendations (for red and white wine respectively), compared with 11.4 per cent of beer drinkers, 5 per cent of rum drinkers and 3.7 per cent of whisky drinkers.

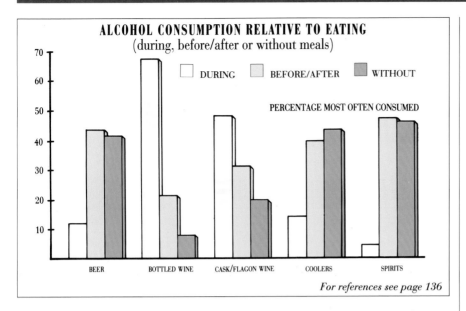

ALCOHOL CONSUMPTION RELATIVE TO EATING
(during, before/after or without meals)

□ DURING   ▨ BEFORE/AFTER   ▨ WITHOUT

PERCENTAGE MOST OFTEN CONSUMED

BEER   BOTTLED WINE   CASK/FLAGON WINE   COOLERS   SPIRITS

For references see page 136

Later research (in October 1990) also highlighted significant differences in the patterns of consumption of wine as opposed to other forms of alcohol. Not only is it more likely to be consumed at home, but is very much more likely to be taken with meals, as the graph (above) shows. The significance of this is twofold: the rate of consumption is slower, and the 'alcoholic effect' is diminished as the food tends to absorb the alcohol prior to it entering the bloodstream. All of this means that the principal risks — underage drinking, drink-driving and excessive consumption leading to violent, antisocial behaviour — are reduced even further in the case of wine. This was recognised as long ago as 1979; a study published in *The Lancet* covering eighteen Western countries analysed the differential effects of different types of alcohol consumption and came down unequivocally on the side of wine.

Where and when

The beneficial effect of moderate wine consumption on cardiac health was first documented in 1904; since that time more than thirty studies involving more than 200 000 people, some conducted over a twenty-year period, have put the matter beyond argument. At the most simple level, those who drink wine are less likely to suffer heart disease than those who do not drink wine (or other alcohol) at all. The most graphic illustration is the comparison of coronary heart disease rates and wine consumption (page 130).

Heart disease

The obvious question is why should wine consumption reduce heart disease. The answer has emerged since 1970, when studies were conducted on laboratory animals and have since been confirmed by repeated studies on humans. We have learnt that those who have high levels of high density lipoprotein cholesterol (HDL) in their blood are protected against coronary artery disease, while those with a high level or high percentage of low density lipoprotein cholesterol (LDL) are particularly vulnerable to this disease. It has now been proved that wine, in small to moderate amounts and consumed regularly, increases the overall level of HDL cholesterol and dramatically improves the HDL to LDL ratio.

Why does wine protect you against heart disease?

129

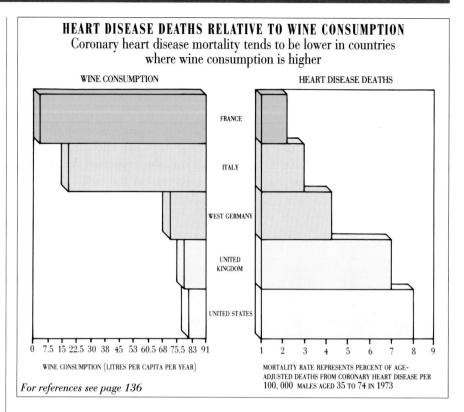

HEART DISEASE DEATHS RELATIVE TO WINE CONSUMPTION
Coronary heart disease mortality tends to be lower in countries
where wine consumption is higher

WINE CONSUMPTION

HEART DISEASE DEATHS

FRANCE

ITALY

WEST GERMANY

UNITED KINGDOM

UNITED STATES

0 7.5 15 22.5 30 38 45 53 60.5 68 75.5 83 91

WINE CONSUMPTION (LITRES PER CAPITA PER YEAR)

1   2   3   4   5   6   7   8   9

MORTALITY RATE REPRESENTS PERCENT OF AGE-
ADJUSTED DEATHS FROM CORONARY HEART DISEASE PER
100, 000 MALES AGED 35 TO 74 IN 1973

For references see page 136

The liver and other digestive organs

When alcohol enters the bloodstream from the digestive tract, it travels first to the liver where it is metabolised. Thus the liver is the first organ to be attacked by excessive alcohol intake, with the initial damage (fatty liver) being reversible, but ultimately causing changes in cell structure, inflammation and the death of tissue. When scar (or dead) tissue replaces liver tissue, cirrhosis has occurred. But according to the limited research available, liver damage does not occur with a daily intake of less than 80 grammes (2.82 oz) or eight standard wine glasses.

Cancer

There is no doubt that those who drink heavily have an increased risk of cancer, although one may wonder at the relative contribution of alcohol and cigarette consumption, given the well-established link between heavy drinking and smoking. At lower levels of consumption, the evidence is unclear. Alcohol per se has not been shown to be carcinogenic; the finger of suspicion is instead pointed at substances commonly found in alcoholic drinks.

Urethane

The current favourite of the neo-prohibitionists is urethane, categorised by the United States Centre for Science in Public Interest (CSPI) as a 'powerful carcinogen'. The CSPI has urged the Food and Drug Administration to cut the allowable level in alcoholic beverages from 125 parts per billion (ppb) to 10–12 ppb with a future target of 5 ppb. Yet even at the present levels a peanut butter sandwich is thirty times as 'carcinogenic' as a glass of wine, a single mushroom 100 times more. Or to extend the examples, a 125 ml (4.23 fl oz) glass of wine with the maximum permissible level of urethane (most wine has much less) is three fourths as carcinogenic as a cup of comfrey herbal tea or a strip of bacon.

Even more popular are the scare games played with pregnant women. It is hard to imagine an easier target. 'I could never forgive myself if I harmed my (unborn) child through my own selfish pleasure. If you cannot tell me there is no risk of any description attached to moderate drinking, I will abstain during my pregnancy.' The fear of the unknown, the innocent victim, and the inherent difficulty — indeed impossibility — of proving the negative form a potent combination: it is not hard to see why so many women these days are choosing not to drink during pregnancy. Even less should they be criticised for doing so; all that one would wish is that they understood the risks and the current state of knowledge.

In one of the most recent books on the subject, *Foetal Alcohol Syndrome* (1990), the author Dr Ernest Abel, an obstetrician and professor at Wayne State University, summarises the profile of the typical FAS mother thus: she has more than ten drinks a day on average; she comes from a low socioeconomic background; she consorts with men who are heavy drinkers; she very probably smokes and has an inadequate food intake; and her overall health is very poor.

It matters not that the level of risk of heavy consumption, measured in terms of FAS births per 1000, is somewhere less than 0.19 per cent (the figures are vigorously disputed). Such behaviour is simply not acceptable, any more than is a single preventable FAS birth. The problem is to clearly define the risk from low to moderate consumption. Thus the Sixth Special Report to Congress (1987) states that the effects from low doses may be real, but are so small that they are difficult to measure.

At the end of the day I come back to the fact that average French and Italian mothers drink five times as much as the average Australian mother, and the rate of foetal abnormality is similar in all countries. I come back to the fact that countless Australian mothers have happily consumed wine during pregnancy with no ill effects. All I can suggest is that the mother-to-be consults her obstetrician, and makes sure she understands his or her advice. If it makes sense, follow it.

Pregnancy and foetal alcohol syndrome

The FAS mother

The levels of risk

What to do

INDEX

135

ACKNOWLEDGEMENTS

PHOTOGRAPH CREDITS
All photographs in this book were provided by Oliver Strewe except as stated below:

George Seper: pp i, v (first two), 11, 12, 13, 34, 37, 40, 60, 61, 62, 68, 69, 70, 73, 76, 81, 83, 90, 91, 92, 94, 96.

Joe Filshie: p 79.

By courtesy James Halliday: p 106 (left)

By courtesy Yalumba: p 117

ILLUSTRATIONS
Grape illustrations by Jenny Phillips

DIAGRAM AND TABLE REFERENCES
Page 52: Aroma Wheel copyright is held by the American Society for Enology and Viticulture; the wheel was developed by Noble, A.C. et al.

Page 128: 1. Turner, T. B., Bennett, V. L., Hernandez, H. 'The beneficial side of moderate alcohol use', *The John Hopkins Medical Journal* 148:53-68, 1981.
2. Jones, B. M., Kingstone, D., Boss, M., Morgan, M.Y. 'Ethanol elimination in males and females: Relationship of menstrual cycle and body composition', *Hepatology* 3(5): 701-706, 1983.
Information by courtesy of *Moderation Reader*, Gene Ford Publications, Seattle, US.

Page 129: Information by courtesy of Winemakers' Federation of Australia.

Page 130: Information by courtesy of American Institute of Nutrition, D. Mark Hegsted and Lynne M. Ausman, *Diet, Alcohol and Coronary Heart Disease in Men.*